THEATR

SCREWED

BY KATHRYN O'REILLY

Screwed was first performed at Theatre503, London,
on 28 June 2016

SCREWED

BY KATHRYN O'REILLY

CAST

Charlene	Samantha Robinson
Luce	Eloise Joseph
Paulo	Stephen Myott-Meadows
Doris	Derek Elroy

CREATIVE TEAM

Director	Sarah Meadows
Designer	Catherine Morgan
Lighting Designer	Jamie Platt
Composer	Benedict Taylor
Assistant Director	Monty Leigh
Educationalist	Tas Emiabata
Dramaturg	Neil Grutchfield
Stage Manager	Polly Heinkel
Design Assistant	Elliott Squire
Prop Maker	Juliet Lano
Production Photography	Hana Kovacs
Flyer and Poster Design	Sophie Sprowell
Press and Publicity	Chloé Nelkin Consulting
Set Build	Away Productions
Rehearsal set built by	Laura Merryweather
	Rhino Scenery
Subsidised rehearsal facilities provided by	Out of Joint

PRODUCTION TEAM

Producers	Kathryn O'Reilly
	& Maeve O'Neill

CAST AND CREATIVES

Samantha Robinson (CHARLENE)

Theatre credits include: *Educating Rita* (Mercury, Colchester); *Untouchable* (Bush); *The Tempest* (Manchester Royal Exchange); *3 Sisters On Hope Street* (Hampstead); *The Phoenix of Madrid* (Theatre Royal Bath); *Dead Heavy Fantastic* (Liverpool Everyman); *The Laramie Project* (Leicester Square); *The Grand Gesture* (Northern Broadsides); *The House of Bernarda Alba* (Nuffield, Southampton); *The Lemon Princess* (West Yorkshire Playhouse); *Song of the Western Men* (Chichester Festival Theatre). TV and film credits include: *Cilla, Island at War, The Girls Who Came to Stay* (ITV); *Five Days, Final Demand, Casualty, Holby City, Doctors* (BBC); *Shameless* (C4). Samantha plays Geraldine in *Footy Pups* for CBeebies.

Eloise Joseph (LUCE)

Theatre credits include: *One Minute* (Courtyard); *Home, Sex Lies and Videotape* (Tristan Bates). TV credits include: *Youngers* (E4); *Coming Up, Skins, Law & Order UK* (C4); *Doctor Who, Vexed, Casualty* (BBC); *Spy, Mad Dogs* (Sky One); *Married Single Other, The Bill, Primeval* (ITV). Film credits include: *The Inbetweeners Movie* (Bwark Productions).

Stephen Myott-Meadows (PAULO)

Stephen is an award-winning actor and writer and co-artistic director of the multi-award-winning Longsight Theatre Company. Theatre credits include work at the Old Vic, Royal Exchange, Pleasance, Bush, Contact, Park and the Lowry. TV credits include: *Life On Mars, Massive, Emmerdale, Hollyoaks*.

Derek Elroy (DORIS)

Derek trained at Rose Bruford College. Theatre credits include: *Routes* (Millennium); *Robin Hood, Kingston 14, Little Red Riding Hood, Aladdin, The Harder They Come 2007* (Theatre Royal Stratford East); *One Man, Two Guvnors* (National Theatre/West End/UK tour); *The Harder They Come* (Playhouse/UK/international tour); *6 Mics No Luggage* (Edinburgh Festival); *Dick Whittington and his Cat* (Barbican); *The World Cup Final 1966* (Battersea Arts Centre); *The Gruffalo* (Tall Stories USA/Canadian tour);

The Blues Brothers (German tour); *666* (Riverside/European tour); *I Was Looking at the Ceiling and Then I Saw the Sky* (Southwark Playhouse/The Royal Opera House); *Big Nose & Mother Goose* (Belgrade, Coventry); *The Adventures of Huckleberry Finn* (Theatre Royal Northampton); *Foe* (Theatre de Complicite tour); *Carmen Jones* (European tour); *Dirty Reality & Forgotten Heroes* (Black Mime). TV credits include: *Fortitude* (Sky); *Rev, If, Casualty, Crimewatch, Hope and Glory, Noel's House Party, Backup* (BBC); *Buried Treasure* (ITV); *The Bill* (Thames Television). Film credits include: *Breakfast on Pluto* (Breakfast on Pluto Productions); *The Diary of Bridget Jones* (Working Title); *The Nutcracker* (Sands Films); *Revolver* (Crucial Films). Radio credits include: *Bad Salsa* (BBC Radio).

Kathryn O'Reilly (Writer & Producer)

Screwed is Kathryn's debut play. As a writer Kathryn was a member of the Royal Court Young Writers Programme and completed playwriting courses with City Lit. Whilst at LAMDA Kathryn won the original poetry writing competition two years in a row. Staged readings of her work include: *Klink Klank Echoes*, as part of Rikki Beadle-Blair's Louder Than Words Festival at Tristan Bates Theatre; *Severed* at Stratford East Theatre Royal as part of Rikki Beadle-Blair's Angelic Tales, supported by Richard Carne Trust; *Caught at Bush Theatre* as part of Rikki Beadle-Blair's Boom! Festival; further development on *Klink Klank Echoes* at Bolton Octagon Theatre, *Poisoned Polluted* at Cambridge Junction; *Scarred*, which had a work-in-development reading at Hampstead Theatre for a scratch night, and further received development from Out of Joint and a reading directed by Blanche McIntyre with a cast including Carey Mulligan, Phil Davis, Celia Imrie, Jamie Forman and Johnny Harris. *Scarred* was longlisted in the top 100 from 2188 submissions for the 2011 Bruntwood Playwriting Competition.

As a producer: *Blood Brothers, The Nutcracker, Top the Pops* and *Little Shop of Horrors* for Mojo at Lewisham Theatre Studio; *Not About Heroes* at Curtain's Up Theatre for MAD House Plays; *Semblance of Madness* at Etcetera Theatre for DameTK Productions. Kathryn produced the short film *Klink Klank* and her own music-and-word events at Tea House Theatre and Tristan Bates Theatre, with Tas Emiabata from Purpleroom Studios with whom she has an EP: *Dame K & Purple T: Rising*.

Kathryn is also an actress and trained at National Youth Theatre, BRIT School and LAMDA. Television credits include: *Holby City, Call the Midwife* (BBC); *Lewis* (ITV); Bafta Award-winning *Random* (Channel 4). Stage credits include, for Out of Joint: *A View from Islington North, Our Country's Good, Andersen's English* and *Mixed Up North*, all directed by Max Stafford-Clark.
kathryn-oreilly.com

Sarah Meadows (Director)

Sarah is an international-award-winning director and Artistic Director of Longsight Theatre Company. Recent credits include: *The Very Perry Show* by Kate Perry (San Francisco International Arts Festival); *Screwed* by Kathryn O'Reilly (Theatre503); *Where Do Little Birds Go?* by Camilla Whitehill (UK tour/ VAULT Festival/Underbelly/Edinburgh Fringe Festival/London transfer; People's Choice Award, 2015 VAULT Festival); *Mr Incredible* by Camilla Whitehill (VAULT/Edinburgh Fringe Festival; winner of the Origins Award for Outstanding New Work 2016); *You* by Mark Wilson (Brighton Fringe; Argus Angel Award, Brighton Fringe Award For Theatre, The Fringe Review Outstanding Theatre Award). In development and staged readings: *Nadya* by Chris Dury, with actors Michelle Terry, Stephen Tomkinson, Phyllis Logan, Shaun Prendergast, David Robb, Dominic Mafham, Rupert Holiday-Evans, Jamie Foreman (Park); *Love in the Moment* (Barbican/Camden People's Theatre).

Catherine Morgan (Designer)

Catherine trained at Nottingham Trent University with a degree in theatre design. Design credits include: *Diaboliad* (Courtyard); *My Story*, *Rise and Fall*, *Ring of Envy*, *Verona Road* (Intermission Youth Theatre); *Twelfth Night* (New Wimbledon Studio); *Othello* (Bussey Building); *Eisteddfod* (Latitude Festival for HighTide); *Baba Shakespeare* (RSC Courtyard/Arcola); *Gerbils in a Glass Cage* (The Space); *Fit for Purpose* (Pleasance, Edinburgh Festival); *Macbeth*, *Hobson's Choice* (Broadway Theatre). As co-designer credits include: *Mr Incredible* (VAULT Festival); and as associate designer: *I Puritani* (Welsh National Opera); *Dido & Aeneas / La Voix Humaine* (Opera North). Catherine has acted as assistant to several renowned designers including: Leslie Travers, Giles Cadle, Stewart Laing, Tom Cairns, Soutra Gilmour, Thaddeus Strassberger, Helen Goddard, Ben Stones and Tim Goodchild. Current assistant engagements include: *La bohème* directed by Richard Jones (Royal Opera House). Catherine works regularly with the National Theatre to develop and lead workshops in theatre design aimed at young people. catherinemorgandesigns.co.uk

Jamie Platt (Lighting Designer)

Jamie trained at the Royal Welsh College of Music & Drama and graduated with a first-class honours degree. He was nominated for an Off-West End Award in 2015 and in 2013 was the recipient of the Association of Lighting Designers' ETC Award and the Philip & Christine Carne Prize from RWCMD. Lighting designs include: *To Dream Again* (Clwyd Theatr Cymru); *Klippies* (Southwark Playhouse); *P'yongyang*, *We Know Where You Live*, *Chicken Dust* (Finborough); *Pattern Recognition* (Platform); *Constellations* (Theatre de Municipal Fontainebleau); *Closer to Heaven* (Union); *And Now: The World!* (Derby/UK tour); *Make/Believe* (V&A Museum); *Ring the Changes+* (Southbank Centre); *The Marriage of Figaro* (Kirklinton Hall/UK tour); *Mahmud íle Yezida*, *BOY*, *Misbehaving*, *The Intruder*, *Bald Prima Donna*, *The Red Helicopter* (Arcola); *One Thousand + 1*, *Fellini: Book of Dreams*, *AnneX*,

QuiXote, Due Saponette Rosse di Tritolo, BURN (Fucecchio, Italy); *Romeo and Juliet* (Pleasance); *The Eulogy of Toby Peach, Mr Incredible* (VAULT Festival); *MICROmegas* (Riverside Studios); *Arthur's Quest* (V45, Edinburgh); *The Children's Hour, Earthquakes in London, Arabian Nights* (Bute); *Once a Catholic, The Merchant of Venice* (Richard Burton). Associate lighting designs include: *The Beggar's Opera* (Park); *The Grit in the Oyster* (Sadler's Wells/world tour); *The Measures Taken, All That Is Solid Melts into Air* (Royal Opera House/world tour); *Our Big Land* (New Wolsey/UK tour). Assistant lighting designs include: *Miss Atomic Bomb* (St. James).

Benedict Taylor (Composer)

Benedict is an award-winning composer and solo violist. He studied at the Royal Northern College of Music and Goldsmiths College, and is a leading figure within the area of contemporary composition and string performance, at the forefront of the British and European new and improvised music scene. He composes, performs and records internationally, in many leading venues and festivals with work being performed/premiered at: the Royal Court Theatre, Rambert Dance Company, BBC Arts Online, Berlinale, Venice International Film Festival, BFI London Film Festival, Toronto Film Festival, Huddersfield Contemporary Music Festival, London Contemporary Music Festival, Aldeburgh Festival, Cantiere D'Arte di Montepulciano, Edinburgh Festival, CRAM Festival, Cafe Oto, Barbican, Royal Albert Hall, Southbank Centre, The Vortex, Ronnie Scott's, ICA, BBC Radio 3 and 2, Radio Libertaire Paris, Resonance FM London. Through his work he is involved with a number of higher education institutions, giving composition, improvisation and performance lectures at the Royal College of Music, City University and Goldsmiths College amongst others. He is the founder and artistic director of CRAM, a music collective and independent record label dedicated to new music. benedict-taylor.blogspot.co.uk

Monty Leigh (Assistant Director)

Monty hails from Warwick, where her career began with the Loft Theatre Company and The Bridge House Theatre Company. She won the Warwickshire Young Directors Award in 2011. She is director/founder of Sharp Scratches, dedicated to supporting new writers by staging their scripts and creating awareness of their work. Monty has experience directing devised and scripted pieces, and has a particular flair for movement work.

Tas Emiabata (Educationalist)

Tas trained as an actor at Rose Bruford College and completed his MA in Applied Theatre at Goldsmiths College. He is a Learning Consultant for Shakespeare's Globe Theatre and regularly facilitates workshops nationally and internationally, training young people and teachers. Tas also works with Talawa, Emergency Exit Arts and has developed and manages Purple Room Studios, an independent production and post-production studio, delivering commissions for the BBC, Crisis, and TENDER, a charity that explores and promotes healthy relationships with young people. purpleroomstudios.co.uk

Neil Grutchfield (Dramaturg)

Neil has a strong interest in and commitment to the development of new writing, developed through his career at the Royal Court Theatre, as New Writing Manager at Synergy Theatre Project, as Literary Manager at Hampstead Theatre, and over fifteen years as a dramaturg and script reader who has worked with first time, emerging, mid-career and senior playwrights. neilgrutchfield.com

Maeve O'Neill (Producer)

Maeve is an independent arts producer, specialising in theatre producing and mentoring. Maeve has produced national tours for poet Simon Mole, Novus Theatre, NIE Theatre and the first production of Blind Summit's award-winning show, *The Table*, at Edinburgh 2011. She works on a regular basis with artists, theatre companies and venues including Ovalhouse, Apples and Snakes, and Jacksons Lane Theatre. She trained at the Gaiety School of Acting, Dublin, and completed a BA in Modern Drama Studies at Brunel University. Current projects include the national tour of *The Diary of a Hounslow Girl* by Ambreen Razia, and Hamswell Festival. maeveoneill.co.uk

Polly Heinkel (Stage Manager)

Polly is a stage manger, director and producer who originally hails from Ohio, in the US. She arrived in London the fall of 2014 to study Directing under the tutelage of Matthew Lloyd at East15 Acting School. She is currently the producer at The Drayton Arms Theatre in South Kensington and has most recently served as Assistant Director to Rikki Beadle-Blair. She is a co-founder of EclecticPond Theatre Company in Indianapolis, Indiana and the Founder and Director of Pollen Productions, which produces productions in both the US and the UK. She is passionate about beginning a dialogue in her work around larger social issues through both classical and contemporary texts. She is excited to be involved with *Screwed* and would like to thank Maeve and Kathryn for this fantastic opportunity.

Theatre503 is the award-winning home of groundbreaking plays.

Led by Artistic Director Lisa Spirling, Theatre503 is a flagship new writing venue committed to producing bold, brave new plays. We are the smallest theatre in the world to win an Olivier Award and we offer more opportunities to new writers than any other theatre in the UK.

THEATRE503 TEAM

Artistic Director	Lisa Spirling
Executive Director	Andrew Shepherd
Producer and Head of Marketing	Jessica Campbell
Associate Artistic Director	Lisa Cagnacci
Literary Manager	Steve Harper
Literary Coordinators	Lauretta Barrow, Nika Obydzinski
Office Manager	Anna De Freitas
Resident Assistant Producers	Kate Powell, Robyn Bennett
Volunteer Coordinators	Serafina Cusack, Simon Mander
Associate Directors	Anna Jordan, Jonathan O'Boyle
Senior Readers	Kate Brower, Brad Birch, Rob Young

THEATRE503 BOARD

Royce Bell, Peter Benson, Chris Campbell, Kay Ellen Consolver, Ben Hall, Dennis Kelly, Eleanor Lloyd, Marcus Markou, Geraldine Sharpe-Newton, Jack Tilbury, Erica Whyman (Chair), Roy Williams.

We couldn't do what we do without our volunteers:
Andrei Vornicu, Annabel Pemberton, Bethany Doherty, Charlotte Mulliner, Chidi Chukwu, Damian Robertson, Danielle Wilson, Fabienne Gould, George Linfield, James Hansen, Joanna Lallay, Kelly Agredo, Ken Hawes, Larner Taylor, Mandy Nicholls, Mark Doherty, Mike Murgaz, Nicole Marie, Rahim Dhanji, Rosie Akerman, Tess Hardy

Theatre503 is supported by:
Philip and Chris Carne, Cas Donald, Gregory Dunlop, Angela Hyde-Courtney and the Audience Club, Stephanie Knauf, Sumintra Latchman, Katherine Malcom, Georgia Oetker, Francesca Ortona, Geraldine Sharpe-Newton.

Support Theatre503
Help us take risks on new writers and produce the plays other theatres can't, or won't. Together we can discover the writers of tomorrow and make some of the most exciting theatre in the country. With memberships ranging from £23 to £1003 there is a chance to get involved no matter what your budget, to help us remain '*arguably the most important theatre in Britain today*' (*Guardian*).

Benefits range from priority notice of our work and news, access to sold out shows, ticket deals, and opportunities to attend parties and peek into rehearsals. Visit theatre503.com or call 020 7978 7040 for more details.

Theatre503, 503 Battersea Park Rd, London SW11 3BW
020 7978 7040 | www.theatre503.com
@Theatre503 | Facebook.com/theatre503

This production is supported by

Philip & Christine Carne
Joanna Bacon
John Stanley
The Richard Carne Trust
Arts Council England
Out of Joint

**ARTS COUNCIL
ENGLAND**
Supported using public funding by

The
Richard Carne
supporting young talent
in the performing arts Trust

The Richard Carne Trust was set up in 2006 to support young
talent in the performing arts, specifically theatre and music.
During this time, it has provided scholarships and financial help
to around 150 young artists. As a supporter of young
playwrights, it is a main sponsor of Theatre503's biennial
Playwriting Award, contributes to production costs of new
drama works, and funds courses for aspiring writers and
directors at regional theatres.

richardcarnetrust.org

out of joint

Inquisitive, epic, authentic and original: Out of Joint develops and produces entertaining theatre that broadens horizons and investigates our times.

Under the direction of Max Stafford-Clark, Out of Joint has premiered plays from established writers including April De Angelis, Sebastian Barry, Richard Bean, Alistair Beaton, Caryl Churchill, David Edgar, David Hare, Rebecca Lenkiewicz, Robin Soans and Timberlake Wertenbaker; launched the careers of others such as Mark Ravenhill and Stella Feehily; and staged bold revivals, most recently a production of Samuel Beckett's *All That Fall* that played to blindfolded audiences and transferred to the West End.

Out of Joint co-produces with the country's most exciting theatres, and its work has been seen in six continents. Future projects include the world premiere of *Consent* by Nina Raine in collaboration with the National Theatre, and a revival of Andrea Dunbar's modern classic *Rita, Sue and Bob Too.*

Out of Joint's Education programme includes workshops, Inset days, summer schools and writing courses, and also incorporates an Associate University Programme.

'The mighty Out of Joint'
Time Out

www.outofjoint.co.uk I @out_of_joint

SCREWED

Kathryn O'Reilly

For Max, Rikki, Gloria & Joe

Acknowledgements
Kathryn O'Reilly

I am extremely grateful to those actors, directors, and venues, who have been part of the readings, development, and who have supported this play over the past five years to get it to where it is today.

Thanks to:

Ramin Gray, Actors Touring Company, Arcola, Pia Furtado, Adam Best, Ovalhouse, Rikki Beadle-Blair, Rebecca Atkinson-Lord, Rebecca Scroggs, Matthew Needham, Pleasance Islington, Gary Beadle, Ciarán Owens, Cassandra Mathers, Hannah Eidinow, Tristan Bates, Theatre Delicatessen, Nathan Ives-Mobia, Lucy Allan, Gemma Lloyd, Act Up, Nadia Nadif, Untold Arts, Nirjay Mahindru, Charlie O'Reilly, Colin Blumenau, The Production Exchange, Cornelius Macarthy, Sarah Meadows, Stephen Myott-Meadows.

All who gave me their support, came to readings, and gave me their generous feedback, including Andrew Alty, Simon Stephens, Timberlake Wertenbaker, John Russell Gordon, Katherine Mendelsohn, Barbara Peirson, Joanna Bacon, Suzette D'Cruz, Kenneth Collard, Alexis Gregory, Mr & Mrs O'Reilly.

Arts Council, Ian Rimmington, Philip and Christine Carne & The Richard Carne Trust, Nick Hern, Sarah Liisa Wilkinson, Karl Sydow, Nicola Seed, Anna Scher, Clean Break.

And from the early days, to Neil Grutchfield for picking and unpicking, analysing character, story, structure, draft after draft, and making me analyse draft after draft. Tas Emiabta for his generosity and support, and through it all, right from the beginning, thanks to Eloise Joseph for such an enjoyable journey and for whom the part of Luce was written for.

All the cast, creative team, and Jackie Malton and Nikki Attree for their generosity and expertise in rehearsals.

All at Out of Joint, Graham Cowley, Panda Cox, Steffi Holtz, Stella Feehily, Jon Bradfield, Martin Derbyshire for his constant support and advice, and Max Stafford-Clark for all his encouragement, reading of many a draft, mentoring and guiding me with his generous questioning and feedback.

Steve Harper and all at Theatre503.

Characters

CHARLENE, *thirty-one years old, female*
LUCE, *thirty years old, female*
PAULO, *thirty years old, half-Russian, male*
DORIS, *fifty years old, Luce's parent, male*

Luce and Charlene talk to the audience as though they are the other characters:

Temp in the Factory
Jonathan in Accounts
Man on the Dance Floor
Man at the Bar
DJ in the Club
Woman on the Dance Floor

This text went to press before the end of rehearsals and so may differ slightly from the play as performed.

Note on Play

Set should be minimal and sparse.

A forward slash (/) indicates when the next line begins.

A dash (–) after a character's name or dialogue indicates an interruption, or an inability to speak.

An ellipsis (…) indicates a trailing off.

A 'beat' means the next line is spoken just that moment too late. It's off the rhythm.

A 'moment' is a lingering longer than a beat.

Prologue

Dance music. We see a short burst of club. Alive, vibrant, full.
LUCE *and* CHARLENE *dancing hard, provocatively, possibly on podiums.*

One

7 a.m. Early morning. A metal factory. Somewhere in West Byfleet, Surrey.

The steel shutters are up allowing us to see directly into the small, grey and cold factory floor. A distant but consistent noise of machinery from somewhere else in the factory. Over that, in this area of the factory, we hear a radio playing club music.

It is the morning after the night before. LUCE *and* CHARLENE, *soulmates, and codependent, still in their clubbing gear underneath their work aprons. Hard-drinking survivors. Worse for wear, but this is standard. They are struggling but with a celebratory feel. They love the fact they can go out all night, get smashed, and come into work the next morning; they live and work to go out.*

They are stood at their stations on the line, working. Putting plastic screw fittings on both ends of braided flexible hosing.

They have been doing this job for so long, they could do it in their sleep.

There is a temp who they are teaching what to do.

CHARLENE   Cold morning.

LUCE   Early morning.

CHARLENE   Every morning.

LUCE   Clocked in –

CHARLENE	Shaking –
LUCE	Radio on –
CHARLENE	Shivering –
LUCE	Kettle boiling –
CHARLENE	Three coffees –
L&C	Blah blah blah –
CHARLENE	Pop the Pro Plus Extra –
L&C	Blah blah blah –

Addressing the temp now.

LUCE	Keep to your station. This is –
L&C	Ours.
LUCE	That is –
L&C	Yours.
LUCE	We go through this demonstration here –
CHARLENE	Here.
LUCE	Then you go over there and you get on with it.
L&C	Right.

Beat.

LUCE	On the line.
CHARLENE	You put your gloves on.
LUCE	I fought for those gloves so you better wear them.
CHARLENE	Not everyone is down the nail parlour twice a week.
LUCE	She wants rough man hands.
CHARLENE	Yeah I do. All over my body.
LUCE	Well the bloke you had last night was as rough as houses.
CHARLENE	What bloke?

LUCE	Best to blank it. (*To the temp*.) Anyway you can thank me for these gloves. Woman power.
CHARLENE	There is something about man's hands, something very manly.
LUCE	There's something about man's cocks. When it's right in front of your face and you're seeing double and you wish there was two! (*To the temp*.) Oh, we're just having a bubble you don't need to have a baby about it. (*To* CHARLENE.) Why did she have to start today?
CHARLENE	Today d'ja know what I'm saying.
LUCE	Face on it. (*To the temp*.) Watch and learn. Temp.

> LUCE *and* CHARLENE *take a breath in, look at each other and go through the demonstration at a lick – stylised movement, demonstrating with the hosing. Not stopping for air, and spouting as if it's one big sentence they've just got to get through.*

	Grab the metal pipe –
CHARLENE	Braided flexible hosing –
LUCE	From that box there –
CHARLENE	Hold it –
LUCE	Firm in your hand –
CHARLENE	Straight –
LUCE	Grab one of them things –
CHARLENE	Fixing –
LUCE	Yeah I know, it's a fixing –
CHARLENE	Fix it to that end –
LUCE	Screw it on –
CHARLENE	I feel –
LUCE	Screw it on –
CHARLENE	I feel –

LUCE	Shut up – you screw it on –
CHARLENE	You gotta get it lined up right otherwise –
LUCE	You get the male bit and screw it in the female bit – simple as –
CHARLENE	Turn it –
LUCE	Other end –
CHARLENE	Fix another fixing –
LUCE	To the other end –
CHARLENE	Check it –
LUCE	Chuck it –
CHARLENE	In the red plastic barrel –
L&C	That's it.

Silence as LUCE *and* CHARLENE *expect applause from the temp.*

LUCE	Right, this demonstration is over.
CHARLENE	You gotta do one of them – (*Indicating the red barrel.*) fill one of them every two hours.
LUCE	Don't compare what you do to us, we've been doing this f–
CHARLENE	For time.
LUCE	Too long.
CHARLENE	I'm gonna be sick.
LUCE	But they won't let us go. Why?

CHARLENE *grabs one of the plastic boxes with the fixing bits in, empties it on the workbench, and ducks behind the workbench, and is sick into the box.* LUCE *carries on working.*

Place would fall apart.
But do get three of them done by lunchtime.

LUCE *watches the temp go to her station.*

Oh no need to thank us.

CHARLENE	My throat is burning.
	LUCE *produces a miniature bottle of vodka.*
LUCE	Hair of the dog, Char.
L&C	Gotta do it to get through it.
	CHARLENE *cracks it open and downs it.*
CHARLENE	I've been in pain all morning and now you tell me.
	LUCE *has a stash of miniatures below their counter, she shows* CHARLENE.
LUCE	We bought 'em, this morning. Twenty-four-hour bargain booze. Keep up. What is that temp eyeballing us for? Temp, you gotta get on with it, can't stand staring in awe at us all day.
CHARLENE	When this morning?
LUCE	(*To temp.*) What is your problem? (*To* CHARLENE.) What is that looking at?
	LUCE *knocks* CHARLENE'*s arm. She flinches and for the first time notices a new bruise, she has no idea where it has come from.*
	She needs it. I don't need this. Now divert those and keep that shut, otherwise I get you sacked.
	LUCE *and* CHARLENE *stare at the temp threateningly.* LUCE *has noticed they are being watched by someone, Jonathan in accounts.*
	Oh here we go. (*Laughing.*)
CHARLENE	What you laughing at?
LUCE	Oh Char, you are hilarious. (*Still laughing.*)
	Jonathan has gone.
	Pervert.
	As if time has slowed down, in slow motion in a dazed and exhausted way, they get on with their job for two minutes, staring out into space not talking – A dull thudding clock ticking out

the monotony as two hours pass at speed in the factory around them.

CHARLENE   I am not doing cocktails again.

LUCE   Heard that before.

CHARLENE   Yeah just sticking to vodka. Straight.

LUCE   I'm having flashbacks here, that Jesus right –

CHARLENE   The one with the beard –

LUCE   Yes.

CHARLENE   And the long hair –

LUCE   Yes.

CHARLENE   What about him?

LUCE   Worst one of the night. Seriously, Char, when I clocked him I thought he's gonna be exiting. You know what they say about a man with long hair. I wouldn't care if he was the only screw I had all night, but nah seriously –

CHARLENE   Where was I?

LUCE   Propping up the bar, I don't know. So anyway, cut a long story short.

CHARLENE   Too late.

LUCE   What?

CHARLENE   –

Beat.

LUCE   He is right up against me, pressing up against me / he's grabbed my hand, next thing I'm off that dance floor, in that toilet –

CHARLENE   Mmm.

LUCE   He's all over me, he's whipped out his cream stick. Whoa.

CHARLENE   Yeah.

LUCE *demonstrates on a bit of hosing.*

LUCE	A grower. He was about as big as this actually, if not bigger, when I saw that, I said to him, you better know how to use that.
CHARLENE	Did ya?
LUCE	I did yeah.
CHARLENE	Did he?
LUCE	What?
CHARLENE	Know how to use it?
LUCE	Disappointment ain't the word. Got the fucking tools don't know how to. He wants to put it up my arse, I'm like 'I don't think so'. So anyway I've got it in my mouth gone for the humming technique, get the vibrations going. Twenty seconds flat, not even, he's shot his lot. I've spat it out. It was like bacon frazzles. I'm like 'What was that? What was that about?' Oh I feel sick thinking about it.
CHARLENE	It's the cocktails, Luce. / Gotta drop the cocktails out.
LUCE	Yeah yeah yeah. So there I am with this time-waster.
L&C	(*Singing.*) T-t-time-waster.
CHARLENE	T-t-time-wast–
LUCE	Yeah. Unsatisfied. So I leave him there, exit the cubicle, I've literally taken one step back on that dance floor and there I am face to face with Will Smith, lookalike, I go 'Fresh Prince, where you been?'
CHARLENE	Bel Air.
LUCE	Exactly. He goes, 'I thought you'd left', I go 'absence makes
L&C	the lust grow stronger'.

LUCE   I'm back in that toilet, different cubicle, he's
            picked me up, like that, I'm up against the door,
            he's up inside me, I am loving it.

            L&C *sing the 'We're Loving It' refrain from
            'Do You Really Like It' by DJ Pied Piper & the
            Master of Ceremonies.*

            I am sensational and he is loving me loving it.
            He's double-shot. Got the stamina. And Jesus is
            outside fucking weeping.
            That's Will Smith off my list.

CHARLENE   He was a lookalike.

LUCE   One step closer, Char.
            Best screw of the night.

CHARLENE   I only got eyes for one man now.

LUCE   Oh please. Paulo. You need to sort that memory
            out. Anyway I thought he was just for a laugh.

CHARLENE   Shut up.

LUCE   You need to sober up.

CHARLENE   What for?

            CHARLENE *cracks open a miniature vodka
            and downs it.*

LUCE   Uugh. Rather you than me. You sure about the
            kebab smell.

            Oh you better gimme one of them. (*Downs a
            miniature.*)

            Time passes at the factory as CHARLENE *and*
            LUCE *continue working.*

Two

Later.

PAULO *enters, in work overalls and steel-toecapped boots, dragging with him an empty barrel, and to roll away the red barrel of hosing that* LUCE *and* CHARLENE *have filled.*

LUCE	You alright, Paulo.
PAULO	Luce. You alright?
LUCE	Yeah.
CHARLENE	You alright, Paulo.
PAULO	Alright, Char.
	There is a moment between PAULO *and* CHARLENE, *before* LUCE *breaks it.*
LUCE	She would be if you forked her.
PAULO	Sorry?
LUCE	She wants a lift on your fork truck.
PAULO	Does she?
CHARLENE	Yeah I think I do.
LUCE	She wants a ride. Please tell me you two ain't done it here. The stink of the metal would do my nut. Here, Char, remember that bloke I fucked last week had a bit of a fetish for the smell of metal?
CHARLENE	Yeah.
PAULO	Luce.
LUCE	Paulo. Oh I know that face.
PAULO	Once in a blue moon I don't mind. You know I don't.
LUCE	Oh here we go.
PAULO	No. It's just, I've got to –
LUCE	Why you only looking at me?

CHARLENE   Got to what?

LUCE   Why you only looking at me when you say all this?

PAULO   It's becoming a habit.

LUCE   Life is a habit, Paulo.

PAULO   It's got to be the last time, you two.

LUCE   Oh god alright. Notice how you sent the temp to me again. As if I ain't got enough to do.

PAULO   You are both falling behind. (*Indicating the half-empty barrel*.) It's not going unnoticed.

CHARLENE   Can I make it up to you?

LUCE   Why is that I wonder. Because I been training her – (*The temp*.) all morning. Am I getting paid extra?

CHARLENE   I don't think so.

LUCE   Who does my job when I'm doing a job that ain't even my job in the first place?

CHARLENE   No one. Paulo, we try our best.

LUCE   Think I might need to speak to the union about it. Training someone is a skill, Paulo. Think about it.

CHARLENE   Did you see *Made in Dagenham*?

LUCE   So I'd watch it if I were you. All of 'em here better watch it.

PAULO   If I get caught.

LUCE   Oh for god's sake live a little, we'd do it for you.

PAULO   You don't have to.

LUCE   Well, she'd do it for you.

CHARLENE   Do I do it for you?

LUCE   Does she?

PAULO   It has to be the last time I clock in for you.

CHARLENE	But not the last time you put your cock in for me.
LUCE	Aaahhh.
PAULO	Char, I'm not joking –
LUCE	Oh fucking hell, dib-dib dob-dob.
PAULO	When you don't hit your target, you put me in an awkward position.
LUCE	She'd love that.
CHARLENE	Is that a promise, Paulo?
PAULO	I've got to put you both on an official warning.
LUCE	Oh please, Char, he'll have to put us on a – (*Singing to the tune of 'Warning' by Fire Fox & 4-Tree.*) warning, warning warning –
CHARLENE	Are you for real?
LUCE	Not one of us any more then.
PAULO	What?
LUCE	You take this job too seriously, Paulo. Ain't he got a stressed-out face, Char.
CHARLENE	Need to chill out.
LUCE	Like you need a good tossing-off. Oh don't get embarrassed it's healthy to masturbate. Stress-busting quick-fix I'm telling you. Char, ain't that right?
CHARLENE	Yeah.
LUCE	Need to relax yourself, get them fingers walking, just go for it now in the toilet if I were you. You could both do with a bit of mutual masturbation, I'll cover.
PAULO	Do you drink every night, Luce?
LUCE	You wanna lighten up, put yourself in an early grave.
PAULO	Way you behave you'll both end up in an early grave.

CHARLENE	I ain't sharing my grave with her.
LUCE	What are you saying?
PAULO	It's just a question.
LUCE	What is your point?
PAULO	Do you?
LUCE	Have I got yellow skin? Do I sleep on a park bench? Have I got broken blood vessels? Have I? Paulo, it's just a question.
PAULO	No.
LUCE	So what was your point?
PAULO	Nothing I'm just –
LUCE	If it's anyone that drinks it's her.
CHARLENE	Yeah.
PAULO	You know if they invented alcohol now it would be class-A.
LUCE	Oh my god.
PAULO	I'm just saying you should be careful. I was reading about breast canc–
LUCE	Paulo, I am living my life. If I wanna go out and party every night, get shitfaced and shag ten men in the toilets then I'm gonna do that. Why?
L&C	Because I can.
LUCE	You think we're Victorians. You think we are gonna sit at home every night –
CHARLENE	Do some knitting –
LUCE	See what I'm saying –
CHARLENE	Putting the dinner on –
LUCE	That's it, Char –
CHARLENE	Dresses to our ankles –
LUCE	Drinking tea –

CHARLENE	Tables have turned –
LUCE	Paulo, we are independent women. We do what we want.
CHARLENE	When we want.
LUCE	How we want. And we ain't taking no shit off no man. Especially a man who used to chill with us, have a bubble, and now thinks he's the boss. Did you actually get a pay rise with your promotion?
	Beat.
PAULO	You both might want to freshen up a bit.
	PAULO *gets on with his work and drags the red barrel away. He exits.*
CHARLENE	Paulo, come on.
LUCE	Char, you wanna up your standards. I'm telling you straight, sexual energy he ain't got and he needs to unblock that second chakra. He ain't got no chat. Look at the way he dresses.
CHARLENE	That's his work clothes.
LUCE	You need to reasses your thinking. And trotters. Tell a lot.
CHARLENE	Thought you didn't mind steel toecaps?
LUCE	On the right man, no. Right situation, no.
	Someone well built. Yes. I'm talking a big back.
CHARLENE	Yeah.
LUCE	Six pack. Which he ain't got.
	CHARLENE *and* LUCE *resume working.*
	See a builder is not gonna be wearing his steel toecaps all day and all night is he. Won't be trudging no muck in my house. See me, *if* I was with him, I'd tell him that like this. 'Leave them in the porch, darling, in your box.'
CHARLENE	Box?

LUCE   Yeah.

CHARLENE   Builder's boots in boxes.

LUCE   On my porch yeah.

CHARLENE   Have you got a porch then?

LUCE   Have I? I have yeah. I got, I got one of these
                chairs does that – (*Gestures*.)

CHARLENE   Swinging chair?

LUCE   Right. I got one of them. I probably got, about,
                three horses, they got an acre each. I got, five
                bedrooms.

CHARLENE   That all?

LUCE   On each landing. Three landings. I got one of
                them, female butler.

CHARLENE   A maid.

LUCE   In waiting, that's you.
                Oh yeah.
                So can't have dirty old steel-toecap boots sitting
                in my porch for all in sorndrey to see.

CHARLENE   'All and sundry.'

LUCE   Exactly. 'Loafers on in the house, darling.

L&C   Outside boots are not coming in.'

LUCE   Any man who can build, imagine the potential.
                Or a business man will do. Can't beat a nice
                whistle.

CHARLENE   Or a man in uniform.

LUCE   Keep your options open. Man's gotta know
                his place.
                Gotta be able to get shot as soon as a better
                model comes along.
                Because a pretty woman with regret ain't
                a pretty picture.

                You getting your nails done tonight?

CHARLENE   No.

LUCE   A man likes a woman looking right. Should
            try it.
            Make an effort.

CHARLENE   I get out of bed in the morning.

LUCE   Little touch up here. Little touch up there. And
            they'll wanna touch you up. We are women,
            born to seduce. Men look at me, they can't help
            themselves. I see it in their eyes.

CHARLENE   I see so many men looking at me.

LUCE   When?

            Beat.

            Jokes.

CHARLENE   I ain't going out tonight.

LUCE   What?

CHARLENE   I'm staying in.

LUCE   You know what's wrong with people? Walking
            around pent-up, angry all the time with their
            frustrated faces.

            World would be a different place. If they just
            got it. On a regular basis. Char, I can't keep
            telling you, you have got to take it wherever,
            and in your case, whenever you can get it. We
            got to get out there. Seriously, Char, I am not
            sitting in your bedsit all night getting pissed
            like two loners. What I'm supposed to do,
            masturbate on me own all night. Nah I need
            satisfaction. YOLO, Char, don't forget. We live
            for the moment, Char, that's us.

            It's an essensuality for humanity to just –

CHARLENE   Make love.

LUCE   Not war.

            Factory bell sounds for lunch.

Three

1 p.m. Lunchtime.

Kitchen of the factory. It's very bare, white, worn and cold, white plastic kettle on the worktop boiling away and microwave turning.

Silence.

Microwave pings, PAULO *gets his food,* CHARLENE *watches him. The kettle finishes boiling.* CHARLENE *makes her coffee with lots of sugar. They sit in silence.*

PAULO	You not hungry?
CHARLENE	Nah.
PAULO	I got plenty.
CHARLENE	I like three cups of coffee in the morning. Come lunchtime.
PAULO	It is lunchtime.
CHARLENE	I'm on four.
PAULO	Need a fix.
CHARLENE	Need a little bit of something yeah.
PAULO	Sure you don't want some?
CHARLENE	Nah you're alright.
	Silence.
PAULO	You're shaking.
CHARLENE	Just cold.
PAULO	You want my jumper?
CHARLENE	Yeah.
	PAULO *undoes his overalls to his waist, takes off his jumper and gives it to* CHARLENE.
PAULO	You know I'm just doing my job, if I don't –
CHARLENE	Paulo, this ain't a career for me so don't worry about it. I'm surprised we ain't been given the elbow.

PAULO	I wouldn't let that happen. To you.
CHARLENE	No but you put me on an official warning.
PAULO	No I just said that coz I can't run the risk any more, I'm walking around tense until you two show up –
CHARLENE	I get it.

Beat as PAULO *moves closer to* CHARLENE.

PAULO	Tonight, I was thinking do you want to… I make a mean stroganoff.
CHARLENE	What like beef stroganoff?
PAULO	Well yeah, beef, yeah, beef is fine if that's what you want.
CHARLENE	Well what other stroganoff is there? Chicken?

PAULO *and* CHARLENE *very close.* LUCE *enters – like a whirlwind bursts into the kitchen – dumps her make-up bag down on the table.*

LUCE	Ooh have I interrupted something. Mmm what is that smell? Smells delicious. What you got?
PAULO	What you want?
CHARLENE	What doesn't she want.
LUCE	Depends.
LUCE	What you offering?
CHARLENE	What you offering?
PAULO	Did I say I was offering?
LUCE	[Is that] From your van?
PAULO	Yeah.
LUCE	Nah.
PAULO	You declining?
LUCE	I'm watching / my figure.
CHARLENE	She's watching her figure.

LUCE	Lemme smell it again. Mmm, that is just... Is it gonna warm me up that's the question? Char, where's my coffee?
CHARLENE	Colombia.
	Beat.
	Jokes.
	CHARLENE *makes* LUCE *a coffee.*
LUCE	(*Re:* PAULO*'s food.*) Oh Paulo, go on give us a bit of that.
PAULO	You want it now.
LUCE	Yeah I want it now and five shugs, Char. It's the way I like it.
PAULO	Is it?
LUCE	Yeah. I prefer it dark. Do you?
PAULO	Erm.
LUCE	Smooth and dark? I love it strong.
CHARLENE	I do.
PAULO	Do you?
	LUCE *sings first line of chorus from 'Coffee' by Supersister.* CHARLENE *sings the second line.*
LUCE	Did I ask for a duet? Ooh give us a bit more.
CHARLENE	Thought we were fasting today.
PAULO	Fasting?
CHARLENE	Oh it's nothing religious.
LUCE	Fuck religion.
CHARLENE	It's just her legs looks like a bomb's hit 'em.
LUCE	I'm gonna let that go coz we all know there is something wrong with you.

CHARLENE	And her fat arse got craters.
	Beat.
LUCE	What yous gassing about then?
CHARLENE	It's alright. Let's talk about you some more.
LUCE	D'ja wanna hurry up with that. My mind is a blank when the caffeine wears down. Heap it up.
CHARLENE	Your mind is often a blank.
LUCE	Oh go and have a wank on your own.
CHARLENE	What?
LUCE	What you showing off for? You're hardly on the planet. You ever seen her, Paulo – you wanna watch her she does this, just zones out, blanks out, you see here when her arms do that – like she's an appoleptic.
CHARLENE	You wanna watch that trap of yours.
LUCE	Oh yeah?
CHARLENE	Have you got any make-up on today?
LUCE	What you saying?
CHARLENE	I'm saying have you got any make-up on today?
LUCE	Bitch.
PAULO	Easy.
CHARLENE	She is, yeah.
LUCE	Experienced.
	Beat.
	You better be coming out with us tonight, Paulo.
PAULO	I don't know.
LUCE	What do you mean you don't know?
PAULO	I don't think I can.
LUCE	What you gotta think about?

PAULO	I gotta be at the van by ten.
LUCE	Oh work work work. After a few cocktails you'll be whizzing round that van, liven things up a bit. Clock off here, straight down bargain booze, little warm-up, you two can watch me get me nails done, hit the town, hit the cocktails, hit the dance floor. Oh Paulo, you have got to seize opportunities.
CHARLENE	You never know if it's gonna happen again.
LUCE	Thank you. Oh my god we was on the bus this morning cudda blapsed this girl right in the boat. She nearly did.
CHARLENE	Paulo this girl's armpit was in my face.
LUCE	I kept my cool. I pressed my nail into the tip of my index finger.
PAULO	What she do?
LUCE	So this is me. I'm standing there. Not a care in the world. I'm telling you seriously, what is a woman – she weren't even a woman, she was a girl, what is a girl doing with a bag like that, on her back yeah, like a terrorist. Whack she goes with it into the side of me.
CHARLENE	Count to three.
LUCE	To ten.
L&C	(*Simultaneous*.) And breathe.
PAULO	(*Simultaneous*.) And breathe.
LUCE	He knows it. I'm like that. I'm looking at her.
CHARLENE	Burning holes / in the back of her head.
LUCE	In the back of her head yeah.
	She realises, I'm like 'what?' she has the aud– aud– audosit–
PAULO	Audacity.

LUCE	Right, to look at me like this.
PAULO	Yeah.
CHARLENE	Like that.
LUCE	Yeah. So I go. 'Do you wanna watch your bag. What?'
CHARLENE	Before I suffocate you with it.
PAULO	You're funny.
LUCE	I know. I said to her, 'You want to respect yourself and just apologise to your elders'. Seriously.
PAULO	You're funny.
LUCE	You said. Oh Paulo. He makes my head spin out. What are they?
PAULO	What?
LUCE	What are you wearing pink socks for?
PAULO	They suit me.
LUCE	Pink socks, Paulo. Nah. Char, you seen them?
CHARLENE	What are you wearing pink socks for?
PAULO	Suit me.
LUCE	Seriously, you're getting too much for me.
PAULO	What, coz of my socks?
LUCE	Where's it gonna end, that's my question.
PAULO	Got them wholesale.
LUCE	I'm not surprised you got them in a sale.
CHARLENE	Wholesale.
PAULO	Bulk-buying, I'm flogging them –
LUCE	Oh you are embarrassing me. You're one of them.
PAULO	One of what?

LUCE	Get your corduroys out like you're living in the seventies.
PAULO	Alright.
LUCE	He'll have a pink napkin sticking out his pocket anytime soon.
CHARLENE	Handkerchief?
LUCE	Who you flogging them to?
PAULO	There's a market for it –
LUCE	Plastic toff.
PAULO	Everyone will always need socks, the demand will never cease.
LUCE	Proper businessman.
PAULO	Giving it a go.
LUCE	Oh you are hilarious, Paulo. You could at least have done make-up. Sort her out with some Éclat. I mean what use to us are you flogging pink socks?
PAULO	It's all about perception. It's all about making people think –
LUCE	What is your perception 'bout a man wearing pink socks, Char?
PAULO	Yeah come on, Char, back me up.
CHARLENE	In touch with his feminine side.
PAULO	Well –
LUCE	Tosser.
CHARLENE	Actually I think they do suit you.
PAULO	Thank you.
CHARLENE	S'alright.
	LUCE *starts touching up her make-up.*
LUCE	Now the question is, are you coming out tonight, Paulo, or not?

PAULO	I don't think so.
LUCE	Well I do think so. All this thinking, Paulo.
PAULO	I can't.
LUCE	I ain't going through this again.
CHARLENE	We're going out for a meal.
LUCE	Nah I ain't going out for a meal.
PAULO	I'm making – we are having a meal together.
LUCE	Having a meal together?
	Beat.
CHARLENE	I am sweating here.
PAULO	You okay?
CHARLENE	Yeah he's cooking for me. Beef strog–
LUCE	Right, how do I look?
	Paulo, how do I look?
PAULO	Better than you did this morning.
LUCE	Better?
PAULO	Yeah.
LUCE	I look better?
PAULO	Yeah.
LUCE	I look sensational.
PAULO	Well –
LUCE	Sorry?
PAULO	Yeah.
LUCE	Right. Time for me to work my magic.
CHARLENE	What you doing?
LUCE	Paulo, I am getting myself that promotion, then we can go celebrate.

CHARLENE   What promotion?

LUCE   Paulo, I am due a promotion. You got a
promotion. Where's mine? Don't ask you don't
get. That's what you men do. Paulo, did you ask
for your promotion?

PAULO   Not really.

LUCE   'Cept I ain't asking. Did Rita O'Grady stand
there and go, no it's alright? Thank you for
paying the men who don't do anywhere near
the amount of work I do, more notes than me.
Did she say that? Right. Plus I need to tick an
accountant off the list don't I.

CHARLENE   Jonathan?

PAULO   Jonathan in accounts?

LUCE   What other Jonathan is there.

PAULO   He's in accounts. / How's he going to give you –

LUCE   I know that, Paulo. He is always perving
over me.

PAULO   He's got a wife.

LUCE   They all have, Paulo. Right. I'll be back in
a minute.

        LUCE *exits*.

PAULO   Did she tell you she was doing that?

CHARLENE   I just had a thought then to pour that boiling
water on my hand.

        Factory bell sounds – end of lunch.

Four

1.45 p.m. After lunch, back on the line.

CHARLENE *is on the factory floor doing her job.*

LUCE is *upstairs talking to Jonathan in the accounts office.*

LUCE   Now, Jonathan, were you trying to put me off
                my work?
                I saw you looking at me down there.
                Wiggling me pipe.
                Is that shirt Paul Smith?
                Really?
                You been working out this morning?
                Pumping iron? Yeah.
                Me? No. Really? You know that I don't.
                Natural.
                Well I like to make an effort. Not that it's much
                of an effort.
                I mean what can you do when you're so close
                to perfection.
                Now, Jonathan, did you do that little thing
                for me?
                Did you put the word in?
                'Process' right.
                Would this be my desk then?
                Watch this, 'Hello, hello, accounts department,
                how may I be of *service*?' Need anything more?

                I was thinking. You've been cooped up here all
                day working hard.

                Can't have that. Two-for-one cocktails tonight,
                blow job, sex on the beach, slow screw. take
                your pick.
                Gimme your number then, I'll tell you where to
                meet me.

Five

Early evening. 7 p.m. DORIS *and* LUCE*'s home.*

DORIS *looking immaculate and* LUCE *and* CHARLENE *are dressed for a night out.* DORIS *is sat in front of a laptop with a webcam, either side of* DORIS *sit* LUCE *and* CHARLENE, *out of shot of the camera. Behind them a big poster of Cleopatra on the wall with red-chilli fairy lights hanging around it. Sensual music is playing in the background.*

DORIS   You are the sexiest woman he has ever seen, and he needs you. He worships you with his whole being. Reveal that cleavage some more. Swoop close to him but don't let him touch. Not yet. His testosterone levels are rising as he prepares himself for you. You run your hands over your chest and get his amygdala gland reacting. His brain will flood with dopamine as you reveal more and more. Signals go to the frontal cortex and this is when you need to have him absolutely in your power.

     Deep breath in and exhale.

LUCE   Mmmm.

DORIS   Mmmm.

     Breathe. You want him to breathe with you, in you, in unison.

     He won't be able to suppress his primal urge. You are stimulating his desire now. Breathe.

     He is putty in your hand. This man wants you now, desperately. You are the miracle he was looking for. Breathe.

     You are his queen.

LUCE   Mmmm.

CHARLENE   Mmmm.

DORIS   The moans of satisfaction. Mmmm.

LUCE   Mmmm. Char, mm.

DORIS	He has a throbbing, throbbing sensation, as you make him physically and psychologically weaker.
	He is now aroused.
CHARLENE	What?
DORIS	He just melts.
LUCE	Do it right.
DORIS	Tease him some more before you go in for the kill. You are thinking, I am Cleopatra.
LUCE	You really get on my tits.
DORIS	Queen of fellation.
	He is now fully erect and you change the rhythm, you apply pressure from the pelvic floor, pull gently alternating hands then it's ten strokes down and ten strokes up. Make sure he is well lubricated.
	Don't forget you enjoy it as much as he does. You are feeling the desire. He enjoys you. And you enjoy him enjoying you. Place his penis in your mouth, gets those lips around his head and start. Any tune will work.
	DORIS *hums 'I'm Every Woman' by Chaka Khan.*
	LUCE*'s phone vibrates with a call.* DORIS *pauses the recording on the laptop.*
	Right, what is going on with you two?
CHARLENE	You said it would take five minutes you know I'm meeting Paulo.
LUCE	And what's your point. Flip. Will this man leave me alone.
DORIS	The man will wait for you. Talk to him later. With tensions rising we need a little TO. Okay. One. Two. Three. And breathe.
	Okay, feeling relieved, tensions gone.

CHARLENE	Thanks, Aunty D.
LUCE	You still paying us for this?
DORIS	I paid you for this last night.
LUCE	That was a loan.
DORIS	Well let's just say I paid you then.
LUCE	What so I got no money to go out tonight? You think I'm stupid, I saw how many views we got last time for 'inner connections', so what's that equate to?
DORIS	You don't even pay me rent.
LUCE	I move out you pay bedroom tax, how's that work out for you. Better still shall I get another loan? Char.
CHARLENE	Luce, I can't afford to get another loan.
LUCE	(*Kisses teeth.*)
DORIS	Right, so let's pick up from where we left off – and we'll just go straight into 'the double-header'. Char, it will take five minutes, if we are all focused.
CHARLENE	You could edit it.
LUCE	I'll edit you.
DORIS	It's live.

DORIS *resumes the live recording on the laptop.*

Aunty D is back, slight technical hitch and of course this is what can happen in the bedroom. Sometimes we have to be patient with our men, sometimes they don't deliver. But when they do. We must praise them. They need it.

CHARLENE	D? What is that smell?
DORIS	Woodbine oil – remember, ladies, to have your woodbine oil burning.

Now. The double-header.

L&C	Double-header.
DORIS	He is erect and you get those lips around it, sucking, this is where your tongue-strengthening exercises come into their own. Licking over the end whilst bringing your fingers of your left hand up, index finger and thumb together, and the right hand down, index finger and thumb together.
	LUCE's *phone vibrates.* DORIS *pauses laptop again.*
	What this is doing for business I don't know, what is wrong with you two? I thought you were serious about this.
LUCE	I am.
DORIS	Looks like it.
	LUCE *answers the phone.*
LUCE	Hello.
DORIS	Luce.
LUCE	Hello, Paul Smith... yeah... I'm getting ready... You wanna know what I'm wearing?
	What?
DORIS	What with you what with her.
CHARLENE	What have I done?
LUCE	That is not what my question is about.
	Oh my god what, you think what? Where you getting off?
DORIS	Sometimes, Char, I think she's –
LUCE	What, think you're big?
DORIS	Someone else's.
LUCE	(*To* DORIS.) You can shut up.
DORIS	Charmed.

Both conversations getting louder as the
dialogue overlaps.

LUCE   (*Back to the phone call.*) You think okay yeah
I can do that, / wot coz she wouldn't have spent
hours –

DORIS   I would have been better off with you as my
daughter.

LUCE   (*On phone.*) Wot / coz she don't mean jack.

DORIS   You woulda been better off with me.

LUCE   (*On phone.*) What coz you think / you're Mister
Big Shot – What? You know what I think,
you're Mister No Shot, it means you're a tosser.

DORIS   This she hasn't learnt from me.

LUCE   (*On phone.*) Mmm, class-A. / A complete tosser.

DORIS   Well, on her mother's side they're all a bit
like that.

LUCE   (*On phone.*) Ain't no other word for you, in fact
I ain't wasting any more of my breath, my time
on you, / I can't even be bothered with you,
don't phone me back, I don't even wanna know
you. I don't know you. I don't even want an
apology…

DORIS   She wasn't a mistake. Straight phase, but
I wanted her.

CHARLENE *blanks out.*

LUCE   (*On phone.*) Ah too late –

DORIS   Char.

LUCE   (*On phone.*) Too late I said –

DORIS   Aunty D to Char.

DORIS *stokes* CHARLENE's *arm.*

LUCE   (*On phone.*) Rejected.

DORIS   Char, I'm here.

LUCE	Don't want it, not accepted… NO… coz it don't mean shit to me. Like you. (*Ends call*.)
	What a dick!
DORIS	You're alright.
LUCE	He's blown *me* out coz his wife's taking him out.
CHARLENE	Yeah.
LUCE	That's it I'll have to come with you to Paulo's.
CHARLENE	He ain't cooking for three.
LUCE	I'm fasting remember.
DORIS	Oh not all that again.
LUCE	Yes all that again, not like I get any food round here.
	LUCE *on her mobile on Tinder to see who can replace Jonathan.*
DORIS	You can cook can't you.
CHARLENE	We'll link with you after.
LUCE	After? (*Swiping phone*.) No. No. No. No. No.
	Right that is it. He's pissed me off, she's pissed me off.
DORIS	You've pissed me off.
LUCE	You piss me off.
CHARLENE	We're all pissed off!
DORIS	Sometimes I wonder where I went wrong.
LUCE	Oh here we go.
DORIS	She breaks my heart.
LUCE	Oh poor me, 'where did I go wrong' parent routine. I've given her everything –
DORIS	Oh don't think you're that special, darling.
	LUCE *exits*.

LUCE	(*Off.*) Well no one could be as special as you. Special needs –
DORIS	Char, would you speak to your mother like this?
LUCE	(*Off.*) She hasn't got one.
DORIS	Well aren't you lucky.
LUCE	(*Off.*) You're an embarrassment.
DORIS	You got your mother's looks.
LUCE	(*Storms back in.*) What did you say? Are you mentally ill.
DORIS	This girl has no decorum.
LUCE	What you bringing the bitch up for?
DORIS	You don't even know her.
LUCE	Nor do I want to. Girl? I am a woman.
DORIS	Well act like one.
LUCE	Like you. As if I ain't got enough to put up with, I've had it my whole life, Char, that, I've had to put up with, that, my whole life. What's your dad like? He's a fucking QUEER.
CHARLENE	What's your problem?
LUCE	You for real?
	Cherry on the cake now he ain't a queer he's a woman trapped. At his age!
CHARLENE	Luce, you ready then?
LUCE	You wanna know what the problem with you is. You're a fuck-up. Day one. (*To* DORIS.) You're a fuck-up, no wonder your mum topped herself.
DORIS	I'd pack your bags if I were you.
LUCE	Don't worry, I'M LEAVING YOU.
DORIS	Do you want some help packing?
LUCE	Well I'm not gonna do it right now am I, I'm going out now, then I'm coming back, then I'm leaving.

LUCE *exits, slamming the door. Blasts music.*

Silence between them as DORIS *goes back to the laptop to answer messages.*

CHARLENE   I think you're brave.

DORIS   Thank you.

CHARLENE   I think knowing what you wanna do, who you are, it's fucking amazing.

DORIS   Charlene, it's taken me my whole life to get here. To be really honest, with myself. Deep down I knew. I knew all along, I was born into the wrong body. When we got pregnant I thought it might make me feel different. Luce's mum had post-natal depression and we tried. I knew it wasn't right to stay, all the time it was there this nagging feeling that everything was wrong. Marriage broke down and eventually she left us. Luce took it hard and ever since I've tried to make it up but I can't. So now I look after me. (*Pause.*) Char, you've got a lot going for you. But you've got to decide what you want.

CHARLENE   Right.

DORIS   You've got to sort yourself out. There's so much more you can do than just working and drinking.

CHARLENE   I'm not sure what you're doing this for.

DORIS   It can change –

CHARLENE   You're making me depressed.

DORIS   It's a dead end you're chasing yourself down. You can choose –

CHARLENE   Doris, you know what I love you to bits you know that. But fuck off.

DORIS   Getting serious with Paulo?

CHARLENE   Getting serious with Andrew?

DORIS   Yeah.

CHARLENE	Good. You told Luce he's moving in yet?
DORIS	No, and don't you tell her, not yet anyway.
CHARLENE	I promised you already.
DORIS	Men choose what they want to see, they need to know they've got what they wanted. Be interested in him, eyes on him. Show him you are just as interesting as you look. Send the signals.
CHARLENE	Right.
DORIS	Keep the energy flowing toward him. And just you remember, you're a queen –
CHARLENE	I'm not –
DORIS	You could be anyone's queen, but you've chosen to spend time with him right now. If he's good enough for you, fair enough. You wanna bring him round I'll give him my rating. No settling for second best. Not for you.
CHARLENE	You're an amazing woman.
	LUCE *enters in a different outfit, throwing* CHARLENE *a clutch bag.*
LUCE	Where's me poppers?
DORIS	What has she got on. / Look at the hussy.
LUCE	Least I dress my age.
	LUCE *is off.*
	Char, are you fucking coming or what! I gotta get me nails done.
DORIS	I'll have some boxes ready for you.
CHARLENE	See you later.
LUCE	You can shove 'em up your dirty shitter.
	CHARLENE *and* LUCE *exit. Door slams.* DORIS *sighs. The lamp with the woodbine oil explodes.*

Six

8:30 p.m. PAULO's home. Living room. PAULO and
CHARLENE sit opposite each other at the table, laid nicely
with candles. Empty dinner plates, almost-empty bottle of wine
– PAULO has some ptichye moloko on a fork to feed
CHARLENE. CHARLENE is topping up her glass.

CHARLENE   What do you mean it's got boiled seaweed in it.

PAULO   Just try it. Go on.

CHARLENE   You better not be trying to poison me.

    PAULO *feeds her.*

PAULO   Good?

CHARLENE   Yeah.

    CHARLENE *continues to eat the dessert.*
    He watches her in silence.

    What?

PAULO   –

CHARLENE   What you looking at?

PAULO   What's your plan?

CHARLENE   –

PAULO   What's your life plan?

CHARLENE   I take each day as it comes, Paulo.

PAULO   I'm retiring come forty.

CHARLENE   That your plan?

PAULO   That's my plan.

CHARLENE   If that's the way you want it.

PAULO   This the way you want it?

CHARLENE   Paulo, I'm thirty-one, I'm not thinking about
    retirement right now.

PAULO   All your thoughts and choices paved your way
    to this day.

CHARLENE	Right.
PAULO	All my thoughts and choices from now on taking me to forty and a charmed life.
CHARLENE	Okay.
PAULO	Go somewhere different, somewhere mysterious where you can just… You know.
CHARLENE	Where's this different, mysterious place you're going?
PAULO	Russia.
CHARLENE	Russia?
PAULO	I'm half Russian.
CHARLENE	I know.
PAULO	It's really beautiful.
CHARLENE	And freezing.
PAULO	I never felt like I belonged anywhere, and the air, I can breathe there. It's about a more simple life you know. I think there are great opportunities for entrepreneurs now, the economy is rebuilding, has rebuilt.
CHARLENE	Not according to Stacey Dooley.
PAULO	Sorry?
CHARLENE	Me and Luce was watching this documentary and Stacey was going round all these brothels in Russia right –
PAULO	Right.
CHARLENE	Well that's it… The brothels was struggling. Sorry, go on. I'm listening.
PAULO	I just felt different there.
CHARLENE	Different.
PAULO	You know, there's a determination in people. I saw it, last time I was there I saw it and I want to be part of it.

CHARLENE	And you've gotta go to Russia to feel different?
PAULO	It's too hard here, Char, I want to have my own building, set up a shop. My shop. Food. Clothing –
CHARLENE	A supermarket?
PAULO	Yeah.
CHARLENE	Paulo's supermarket.
PAULO	I'm thinking, well I've planned that I'm going in a month.
CHARLENE	In a month?
PAULO	Selling my van.
CHARLENE	What you gonna do, put it on eBay?
PAULO	Yeah.
CHARLENE	Right so you're going going yeah? In a month you're off. And you're telling me now.
PAULO	And you could come.
CHARLENE	Is that your plan for me?
PAULO	What's stopping you?
CHARLENE	Paulo, I like my job. It's funny, I do. I'm alright there.
PAULO	You don't wanna work there till you're seventy.
CHARLENE	Who would?
PAULO	Got anything to lose?
CHARLENE	Well this is, this is really nice. This could be your send-off meal.
	You know what, Paulo, I think it's a great idea, you know –
PAULO	Yeah –
CHARLENE	Yeah I could come 'n' all.
PAULO	Yeah?

CHARLENE   Yeah. This deserves celebrating.

*CHARLENE downs her glass and pours
another for herself and one for PAULO.*

Cheers or whatever the fuck they say over there.

PAULO   *Ypa.* [Ura.]

CHARLENE   *Ypa.*

*They cheers. She drinks and moves in, kissing
PAULO, getting more intense she tries to
undress him.*

PAULO   Char. This is –

CHARLENE   What, Paulo – you gotta seize the opportunity.

PAULO   Come on, I've got –

CHARLENE   What you got? You got me in front of you right
here, right now. And if you are going this is it –

PAULO   We've got time, especially if you're coming.

CHARLENE   Be serious.

PAULO   I thought –

CHARLENE   Paulo, I don't know anything about Russia.
I'm not a travelling person. I'm not. You know,
I mean, you're crazy. I mean it's your dream
and that's, that's amazing.

CHARLENE tries to undress PAULO again.

PAULO   Char, come on –

CHARLENE   You come on, Paulo. Ain't that what this is
about? Don't tell me you don't want a shag.

*He pushes her off him – rougher than he
intended.*

Moment.

CHARLENE's mobile rings.

We better get going.

PAULO   You haven't finished your –

CHARLENE   She's waiting for us, so we better get going.
             Paulo, this was, really, it was… You, you're
             a great cook. Yeah, yeah, Paulo, no you are,
             fucking amazing.

Seven

*10 p.m. Evening. Woking town centre. The toilets of a small
nightclub, which is more like a bar with a dance floor. The
music is pumping.*

LUCE *is on the toilet.* CHARLENE *is staring at herself in the
mirror, drinking what is left of a small bottle of vodka they've
smuggled in.*

LUCE   Stop looking in the mirror, you'll only feel
             worse.

CHARLENE   I'm not looking in the mirror.

LUCE   I can hear you.

CHARLENE   Looking in the mirror?

LUCE   Told ya.

             Oh Char, did you not see Big Brian, seriously,
             he's old enough to be my granddad. Fucking
             dirty old man. Trying to touch me up in the
             cloakroom queue. Like I want a sugar daddy.
             Did you see him?

CHARLENE   You gonna be all night in there?

LUCE   The man will wait for you.

CHARLENE   I'll meet you out there.

LUCE   Oh my god, I'm pulling up my knickers,
             alright. Anyway what you 'avin'?

CHARLENE   Whatever, don't matter does it. Long as there's
             enough of it.

LUCE	You got any of that vodka left?
CHARLENE	No.
LUCE	You rinsed it already?

CHARLENE *downs the last of the vodka.*

LUCE *comes out of the toilet, straight to the mirror, checking herself.*

Char?

CHARLENE	What.
LUCE	Char?
CHARLENE	What.
LUCE	The key is, key is you gotta use the man.
CHARLENE	Don't let the man use you.
LUCE	Don't let the man use you.
CHARLENE	Don't let the man use you.
LUCE	Thank you.
LUCE	They all make promises.
CHARLENE	Quick at making promises.
LUCE	Then don't deliver, does my head in.
CHARLENE	Makes me wanna kick their heads in.
LUCE	Exactly. Give the benefit of the doubt and you let yourself down.

You need to touch that lipstick up. Come here.

LUCE *applies lipstick to* CHARLENE*'s mouth.*

(*To herself in the mirror.*) Looking sensational.

CHARLENE	Looking –
LUCE	Gonna get that man.
CHARLENE	I am gonna get that man and make him cum all night.

LUCE	Have you made a man cum before though, Char.
CHARLENE	You wanna watch that trap of yours.
LUCE	Jokes. What are you so tetchy about? Oh my god, I know.
CHARLENE	What?
LUCE	No don't worry about it, but I know.
CHARLENE	What the fuck do you know?
LUCE	Didn't get any after all?
CHARLENE	You know nothing.
LUCE	I think you need to relax yourself. I think it's popper time for somebody.
	Proper popper time.
CHARLENE	Pretty proper popper time.
LUCE	Propper popper time.
	LUCE *gets a bottle of poppers out of her bag, does some and passes to* CHARLENE.
	Inhale.
CHARLENE	Right. Inhale.
LUCE	Deep. Get the blood flowing.
CHARLENE	Head rushing. Instantly.
LUCE	Inster... tainiously. Blood pumping.
CHARLENE	Feels like my head's gonna –
L&C	Pop.
LUCE	(*Singing.*) Getting on one. Proper getting on one.
	Right. Men.
CHARLENE	Right.

LUCE	Men.
CHARLENE	Men.
LUCE	Yes. Men.
CHARLENE	Yes, men.
LUCE	Cock.
CHARLENE	Yes
LUCE	Cock.
CHARLENE	Yes
LUCE	Cock.
CHARLENE	Yes
LUCE	Cock.
CHARLENE	Yes
LUCE	Cock.
CHARLENE	Yes
LUCE	Cock.
CHARLENE	Yes
L&C	Cock!

They exit the toilets.

Dance floor. The music is loud. Lights. A full club. They strut their way straight to the centre of the dance floor.

LUCE	DJ!
CHARLENE	Dee Jaay!
LUCE	Watch my move, wanna watch my move.
L&C	(*Singing.*) Wanna watch me? Watch me. Wanna watch me?

They dance their rehearsed routine provocatively as if everyone in the club is watching them.

LUCE	Look at him looking at me.
	Char, ten o'clock you got one.
CHARLENE	Who?
LUCE	Him.
CHARLENE	Who?
LUCE	Bit pissed though.
CHARLENE	The pissed one?
LUCE	Oh he's looking at me now. Do you want her or me?
CHARLENE	If I do this, is he still looking at me?
	CHARLENE *is thrusting her chest back and forth at the man looking at her.*
	PAULO *enters, comes over with drinks.*
PAULO	Where've you been?
	PAULO *kisses* CHARLENE.
LUCE	Perfecting the beauty that is radiating right now in front of your face.
	Where've you been more like. Lucky I had Stephen Chong down the nail parlour, and he gave me fifty per cent off, what do you think?
PAULO	Yeah.
LUCE	(*Kisses teeth.*)
PAULO	Here – (*Handing over the drinks.*)
LUCE	'Bout time. I nearly died of withdrawal.
CHARLENE	*Ypa!*
PAULO	*Ypa!*
LUCE	What-ra?
PAULO	I've gotta go soon.
CHARLENE	Dance with us.
PAULO	I am dancing with you.

LUCE	Move. I got one watching me, drooling – What's that?
PAULO	What you asked for.
LUCE	I can't taste any alcohol in that.
PAULO	It's what you asked for.
LUCE	Give me some money, I'll go to the bar myself.
PAULO	You don't like it?
LUCE	No.
PAULO	You don't like that drink?
LUCE	Look, I don't like it, she don't like it. What is your problem?
CHARLENE	I don't mind it.

CHARLENE *pulls* PAULO *into her, holding his gaze – they are in a world of their own.*

LUCE	I really haven't got time for this. Char, do you want this shit? She'll drink anything that one. Char!

PAULO *and* CHARLENE *are kissing.*

How can you get a fucking cocktail wrong? Seriously. Oh here we go, Char, three o'clock. Three o'clock Jack, in the sack.

LUCE *exits in pursuit of this new man at the bar.*

Dance floor. PAULO *and* CHARLENE *dancing.*

CHARLENE	Want some? (*Gets out the bottle of poppers.*)
PAULO	I haven't done these since I was at school.
CHARLENE	Instant rush.
PAULO	Wears off quick.
CHARLENE	Everything wears off quick. Everything's fleeting. But just a moment.

PAULO	A moment?
CHARLENE	Yeah.
PAULO	Yeah?
CHARLENE	The buzz in your head when you're dancing.
PAULO	Yeah?
CHARLENE	The rush
PAULO	The rush.
CHARLENE	Ruuusshh.
PAULO	Ruuusshh.
CHARLENE	Ruuushing in Ruusha –
PAULO	Ruusha –
CHARLENE	It's like it there's no… it's just for here.
PAULO	This moment.
CHARLENE	Then it's gone.
PAULO	Look it's not that I didn't want to right.
CHARLENE	Yeah and what about the time before then?
PAULO	Char, I can't just, it's got to be right.
CHARLENE	When is right, Paulo?
PAULO	You know what I mean.
CHARLENE	I'm not the one leaving in a month.
PAULO	I'd like to, but…
CHARLENE	But?
PAULO	It's getting late.
CHARLENE	I see.
PAULO	I've really gotta go…
CHARLENE	Yeah…
PAULO	Want to stay but I.

CHARLENE   You do what you want to.

PAULO   Don't be like that.

CHARLENE   I'm not being like anything.

PAULO   Come to my van on your way home, I'll give you a bite.

CHARLENE   Oh yeah?

PAULO   Yeah.

CHARLENE   One for the road?

CHARLENE *kisses* PAULO.

LUCE   I've met men like you before.
You trying to have the power.
What?
What are you questioning me for?
One too many? I've had one not enough.
This was a dare, talking to you.
Oh yeah big man.
You disgust me.
Why do you hate yourself so much?
See them yeah, they're my mates. He's Russian and she's a fucking cage fighter.

PAULO *kisses* CHARLENE *goodbye and exits.*
CHARLENE *heads over to* LUCE.

You're the dirty ugly twat.

CHARLENE *is there.*

(*Gasps.*) What you calling her ugly for? Bet you can't even get it up. Total fucking time-waster from the start.

CHARLENE   Time-waster?

LUCE   Blatant time-waster.

L&C   (*Singing.*) T-t-time-waster. T-t-time-waster!

LUCE   Yeah go on coz she'll basically kill you if you don't fuck off.

CHARLENE   Fuck off.

Eight

12:30 a.m. Still at the nightclub. Later, LUCE *and* CHARLENE
are off their faces.

*Stylised movement as time passes – they down shots. Attempt to
do their rehearsed routine ritual dance again – but this time out
of time with each other.*

LUCE	I've had enough of this farmyard. What the fuck is that looking at?
CHARLENE	What is she about?
LUCE	State. Yeah. Yeah you, you slut.
CHARLENE	State of it.
LUCE	What does she look like?
CHARLENE	Mess.
LUCE	Face like the back end of a face like a –
CHARLENE	Prick.
LUCE	She wants to stay outta my way. I need a drink. Where's Paulo?
CHARLENE	Kebab van.
LUCE	Well he's another one.
CHARLENE	What is he snogging her for?
LUCE	Son of a – (*Shouting across the dance floor to the couple.*) Wasting your time, luv. Yeah. You. Bum-bandit.
CHARLENE	(*To the woman.*) What?
LUCE	(*To the woman.*) Slag.
CHARLENE	I got your back.
LUCE	Seriously, Char, it won't be pretty but it will be an improvement. What is she looking at us with her frustrated face for? See her. (*To the woman.*) You have got the stamp of tramp all about you. What? Z-list skank rank slapper.

CHARLENE	You heard.
LUCE	Oh yeah. What?
CHARLENE	Coz you think you're –
LUCE	What?
CHARLENE	Get trotting.
LUCE	You heard.
	She is so facesty. If she looks at us again. I will knock her out. Char.
CHARLENE	I will knock you out, slag.
LUCE	What the fuck are you looking at?
CHARLENE	What the fuck are you looking at?
LUCE	Don't think we won't.
CHARLENE	Is she stepping up?
LUCE	(*Squaring up to this woman.*) I'm warning you, tramp. Oh my god, you wanna go epilate your face.
CHARLENE	I will screw you up.
	The woman pushes LUCE.
LUCE	Touch me again.
CHARLENE	Touch her – (*Pushes the woman back.*) touch her again I will batter you.
	You and your slag shit mates
LUCE	Touch me, bitch.
CHARLENE	Try me.
LUCE	We will ruin you.
CHARLENE	TRY ME.
	I will smash you up.
LUCE	Mash you up.
CHARLENE	I will bash you up.

LUCE	I'll put you in a coma.
CHARLENE	I will screw your fucking life up –
LUCE	Bitch. I will stab your face up with my heel.
CHARLENE	Bitch.
LUCE	Bitch. Bitch. Go on, Char. Stab that cunt's face up.
	CHARLENE *savagely attacking the woman with the heel*.
CHARLENE	Bitch. Bitch. Bitch. Bitch. Bitch. Bitch. Bitch.

Nine

Later. 1 a.m. High street. Woking.

PAULO in his kebab van, cleaning his surfaces, he finishes and starts reading Retail Week *magazine. It's a quiet night.*

Offstage, LUCE and CHARLENE can be heard from down the street, shouting, shrieking and laughing. A car beeping at them.

LUCE	Ah whaaaat.
CHARLENE	Whaaaat.
LUCE	Drive on.
L&C	Driiiivee.
LUCE	Paulo.
CHARLENE	Paulo.
L&C	Pauuulooo!
	LUCE *and* CHARLENE *get to* PAULO*'s kebab van.* LUCE *is barefoot and carrying one of her heels.* CHARLENE *has a bottle of vodka in her hand. They are obliterated, also adrenalin-fuelled and triumphant.* CHARLENE *has bloodstains on her dishevelled clothes. They are*

very animated and at first PAULO *is swept up*
in their energy and excitement. They hardly
stop for air as they barrage PAULO *with their*
story, talking over him.

LUCE   Oh my god, you –

L&C   – missed it!

LUCE   Paulo, you missed it.

PAULO   What?

CHARLENE   Paulo –

LUCE   Some slapper slut tramp proper fu–

CHARLENE   Right –

PAULO   Right –

LUCE   We were like –

L&C   You wanna back off –

CHARLENE   Bitch –

LUCE   Bitch –

PAULO   Yeah.

LUCE   One of them, should have been terminated –

CHARLENE   And the mother for having it –

LUCE   Fuck so ugly –

CHARLENE   Fugly –

LUCE   Yeah you wanna throw up –

CHARLENE   Shit on it.

PAULO   Agggh.

LUCE   Some bloke seducing –

CHARLENE   She's, this bloke –

LUCE   Me right, the tramp pipes up, you listening?

PAULO   What are you both on?

LUCE   She was on a jealous rampage.

CHARLENE	Paulo, she was a slut.
LUCE	What am I on? Seriously I drunk so much I'm probably sober.
CHARLENE	This woman –
LUCE	The tramp slut –
CHARLENE	Stepped up –
LUCE	She weren't no woman, she was a girl –
L&C	How old was she?
CHARLENE	Ten –
LUCE	Looked a hundred an'…
CHARLENE	Giving it / provoking us –
LUCE	With the lip, with the eye, he was babbling it / some shit –
CHARLENE	Babbling it –
LUCE	Getting closer, we haven't even done nothing right, nothing –
CHARLENE	Zero –
LUCE	Before she, in my face –
CHARLENE	I've / weaved in –
LUCE	[She's] Done that, the bitch is, up / my face –
CHARLENE	Push that bitch –
	CHARLENE *has lost herself, rage seething out of her, reliving the fight, physically demonstrating – it is an ugly, frightening sight.*
	'Stead of trotting –
LUCE	She's like – up for more –
CHARLENE	That in my face now –
LUCE	In her face, bring it –
CHARLENE	Bring it, had to land a couple – bam –
LUCE	Bring it –

CHARLENE	Bam –
LUCE	Shoulda seen that girl, Char knocked her right out, she was like –
L&C	Bam –
LUCE	The tramp went down –
L&C	Bam –
LUCE	Bam her eye just went out like that, puffed up, I was like, wiv my drink, 'ave it, wasted a drink on it, flip –
	Over the imaginary woman they are beating up.
CHARLENE	Bitch, I will rip your mouth apart –
LUCE	Yeah.
CHARLENE	I will break every bone in your face up.
LUCE	Right I've just had this fight break out over me, all I was doing was standing there, and all of sudden carnage.
PAULO	You alright?
LUCE	I'm alright yeah. But she took one you took one didn't you.
PAULO	I wasn't asking you.
CHARLENE	I'm alright. Yeah.
LUCE	Proper tight, don't mess with us.
PAULO	Did you not take one then?
LUCE	Oh Paulo, I love the smell of that.
PAULO	Do you?
LUCE	Ooh I love the sound of that. I love the sound of sizzling, meat.
PAULO	You alright?
LUCE	She said yeah. Talk Russian to me. Come on.
PAULO	You need to calm down.

LUCE	You need to calm down, what is your problem? Anyway, what are you offering? Let's see some of these businessman skills. What is that? Bon, bonna, boner kabab, have you got a boner kebab?
CHARLENE	Donner. Who's heard of a bonna kebab?
LUCE	Well he wants to make that clearer. Paulo, I am waiting, what's this?
PAULO	Donner kebab, lamb shish, chicken shish, chips, or a juicy fat burger all the trimmings, salad, cheese, peppers / make it hot, or a full and flavoursome special –
L&C	Poppers!
PAULO	Peppers. Mixed-meat kebab.
LUCE	Is it juicy?
PAULO	As juicy as you want it.
LUCE	Stop it. Can you make it hot 'n' spicy?
PAULO	If that's what you want.
LUCE	It's what I want.
PAULO	If that's the way you like it.
LUCE	That's the way I like it.
CHARLENE	That's the way she loves it.
LUCE	Ignore her.
PAULO	Well if that's what you want and that's the way you like it.
CHARLENE	I'll have a donner thanks, Paulo.
	PAULO *makes the kebab during the following.*
PAULO	I like a woman who can make a decision.
LUCE	I can make a decision. I just like to take my time, considering the options.
	Beat.

Give us a try of that hot 'n' spicy, fat 'n' juicy –
Just gimme a sliver. It's doing my nut just
watching it, sweltering. Paulo!

He cuts meat off and LUCE *opens her mouth
expecting him to feed her. He doesn't. He puts
the sliver on a paper napkin and gets on with*
CHARLENE*'s kebab.*

LUCE *picks it up and plays with it, dangling it
above her mouth, finally eating it.*

Oooh, that is…

Talk to me in Russian.

CHARLENE	Luce, drop it out.
LUCE	Who threw you nuts?
CHARLENE	What?
PAULO	Salad? Char, salad?
CHARLENE	Yes.
LUCE	What?
CHARLENE	Carry on.
LUCE	Oh my god I'm only having a laugh. Is someone getting a bit jell?
CHARLENE	Getting a bit jell?
LUCE	Getting a bit well-jell – ugh, you just need to take you and your little fucking massive jealousy. / Anyone can see a mile down the street, away from me.
CHARLENE	Jealous of you. I feel sorry for you.
LUCE	Oh sounds like it. Get yourself away from me.
CHARLENE	Was you invited here?
PAULO	Come on, you two, / you'll be driving my customers away.
LUCE	What customers.
CHARLENE	Did you invite her here?

LUCE   Do I need an invitation?

PAULO   We've all had a long night.

CHARLENE   You ain't wanted.

PAULO   Come on, girls.

LUCE   I'm a woman. Another thing, where's my shoe?

CHARLENE   Up your arse.

LUCE   Up my wha-what? You better be getting me
              some new heels.

CHARLENE   Get your / own.

LUCE   First thing I want them, I want them first thing,
              on my desk.

CHARLENE   Oh is that the desk, is that the promotional desk
              you got then –

LUCE   Ahhhh.

CHARLENE   – from Jonathan who fucking blew you out –

LUCE   Does he even know who you are?

CHARLENE   What's that now. Three nights in a row. Jonathan,
              failed. Jesus, failed. Who d'ja, who d'ja, who'd
              you get fuck tonight? No one. Failed.

LUCE   Everything I – notice that, Paulo, everything I –
              you want this, here have this.

              LUCE *throws her heel at* CHARLENE, *she
              misses.*

CHARLENE   What are you testing me for?

LUCE   Paulo, Paulo.

PAULO   Peppers? Char?

CHARLENE   Nah.

LUCE   She can't take it hot.

PAULO   I bet she can.

LUCE   What?

CHARLENE	What?
LUCE	You, you can't take it hot, bland and boring that's how she has it.
CHARLENE	I don't like chilli peppers.
PAULO	You haven't had mine yet.
LUCE	Yeah and nor does she want to.
CHARLENE	Maybe I do.
PAULO	Do you?
LUCE	No she don't.
CHARLENE	Yeah I do.
LUCE	What for?
CHARLENE	Maybe I wanna try him – his peppers.
LUCE	A chilli pepper is a chilli pepper, ain't nothing special about his.
PAULO	When was the last time you had one?
LUCE	She's never had one.
CHARLENE	Haven't I?
PAULO	Do you want one?
CHARLENE	Yeah.
LUCE	You just said you don't like them.
PAULO	Open up.

PAULO *gets a chilli and dangles it above* CHARLENE*'s mouth, she puts her lips around it, bites it to the stem eating it whole.*

CHARLENE	I like it.

Beat.

Can I have that kebab now?

PAULO	Chilli or garlic?
CHARLENE	Garlic / sauce, no –

LUCE	Garlic. Told ya.
	PAULO *puts the garlic sauce on the kebab and places it on the counter for* CHARLENE.
PAULO	Here you go.
CHARLENE	Ah Paulo.
PAULO	Yeah?
CHARLENE	That is just what I wanted.
PAULO	Yeah?
CHARLENE	Yeah.
	Silence. CHARLENE *starts eating the kebab.*
PAULO	You decided?
LUCE	I wanna see your kitchen. I do, yeah. I insist. You know a customer can ask to inspect any kitchen before trying the food. Says a lot about the chef, how tidy the kitchen is.
PAULO	As you can see it's a very clean kitchen, very tidy kitchen and I have my hygiene certificates.
LUCE	D'you get 'em off eBay?
CHARLENE	Shut up.
LUCE	It's a joke.
PAULO	It's okay. And my surfaces are spotless.
LUCE	I can't see your floor from down here though. I need to make an inspection of your clean and tidy, hygienic kitchen, Paulo. Chef. Chef.
	LUCE *walks round to the van door at the side, enters it, closes the door.*
	That certificate better be right.
PAULO	Luce, you need to –
LUCE	(*To* CHARLENE.) Wait for me.
CHARLENE	Paulo, you got a toilet?

PAULO	No.
CHARLENE	Why ain't you got a toilet? Ain't you got a portaloo?
PAULO	No.
CHARLENE	Open up your back door, make a cubicle for me.
PAULO	What? No.
CHARLENE	What's wrong with you?
PAULO	You can't come in here. I make food in here.
CHARLENE	I'm not talking 'bout coming in am I, just open the door. Luce, open the door.

CHARLENE *is hitching up her skirt.*

PAULO	Char, Char, what are you doing?
LUCE	Aahhh.

CHARLENE *has squatted and is pissing in the street by the side of* PAULO*'s van.*

CHARLENE	What is your problem?
PAULO	You.
CHARLENE	Oh right.
PAULO	Char, have some dignity.
CHARLENE	Like you?
PAULO	That is dirty.
CHARLENE	I'm the dirty one.
PAULO	Yeah, that is dirty / you're a woman, act like one.
CHARLENE	Greasy little caravan. He's opening some –
PAULO	Fuck off, go on.
CHARLENE	You taking this greasy caravan to Russia? Oh yeah no he's leaving us. Fucking great plan. Making your millions in your caravan supermarket. That's his plan. Luce, he's got a 'life plan'.

PAULO   You better fucking go, Char.

CHARLENE   Or what? She says you stink of kebab meat.

LUCE   No I didn't –

CHARLENE   Oh she's piped up. What you taking his side for?

PAULO   You are disgusting. You are a dirty –

LUCE   Paulo, chill out –

PAULO   Go home.

CHARLENE   Fffffff.

PAULO   You are an embarrassment.

CHARLENE   So are you.

               PAULO *brings down the hatch of his kebab
               van shut.*

               Have your fucking kebab, it tastes of shit.

               CHARLENE *throws the kebab, and the vodka
               bottle at closed hatch of the van.*

               Fuuuck you're virtually an immigrant, you take
               two jobs and what you doing? Leaving the
               country with the money. Fuck you. Fuck you.
               Fuck you.

Ten

2 a.m. LUCE *and* PAULO *in* PAULO*'s kebab van.* PAULO
slightly shell-shocked and furious with CHARLENE.

LUCE   Don't worry about her. She does this. She'll
        calm down.

        It's a shame, coz she likes you, you know,
        likes you.

        Does it get boring in here?

PAULO   Hardly.

LUCE   What's this for then?
        Does this suit me?
        Put some onions on there, push 'em around as
        they sizzle. I love that. Sizzle.

PAULO   Don't waste my food.

        Steam comes up from the onions in LUCE*'s face.*

LUCE   Oh it's a bit hot in here isn't it.

PAULO   Have you seen my floor now? (*Moves the
        onions and moves her out of his way.*)

LUCE   What's the rush?

PAULO   I think you better go.

LUCE   Ooh that is grea–

PAULO   Can you not –

LUCE   I'm just 'aving a go –

PAULO   Touch that –

LUCE   Oh what's this? Ketchup. Do you make much
        money here then?

        LUCE *is all over the place as she's looking at
        everything, picking things up. She grabs some
        bread buns and puts them up against her chest.*

        What do you think of my buns, Paulo?

PAULO   Put my buns down.

LUCE   You need to chill out.

            LUCE *undoes his apron that is tied around his waist at the front.*

PAULO   What you doing?

LUCE   (*Putting his apron on.*) Come on, shop's shut ain't it. I bet you you'd rake it in if I was here. If I was here doing this. Just standing here. What do you reckon? Paulo, I have to say, this van, you've got it pretty, you've got it all in here. I could do this.

PAULO   You think?

LUCE   No sweat. Seriously. How much you make you reckon? I will triple it in a minute. I'll tell you what we could really make something of this. Me here, taking orders, you there, flipping your burgers. We could turn this place around.

            LUCE *slips as she replaces the buns.* PAULO *catches her.*

PAULO   Whoa. You alright?

            There is a moment between the two of them, PAULO *holds* LUCE *to him.*

LUCE   What? Oh nah.

PAULO   I'm gonna call you a cab.

LUCE   Oh my god, you like me.

PAULO   Luce, step outside.

LUCE   Oh my god.

PAULO   What?

LUCE   You like me. All makes sense now. You are always touching me –

PAULO   Right, get out. Luce. Get out.

LUCE   Nah, Paulo, that's not right. (*Taking off his apron.*) Char! I'm not having men like you coming on to me.

LUCE *beats* PAULO*'s chest with her fists,*
pushing to get past him.

I've 'ad it up to here tonight.

PAULO   Stop it, Luce.

LUCE   (*Shouting*.) Char!

Snap to black.

Eleven

2 30 a.m. Later. Empty multistorey car park in the town centre.
LUCE *lying on the ground, in some pain, cradling one hand*
close to her chest, slurring her words. CHARLENE *staggering*
about and throwing up. Both paralytic.

LUCE   I'm having
            Fucking
            Oh my god.

CHARLENE   Uurrgh.

LUCE   I'm not alright you know. You know…
            Why is the floor moving?
            Earthquake? Oh my go(d) – oh my go(d) my,
            my oh my god my nails. Look, look look, state
            of – Melted.
            Look.
            What am I supposed do… like? Like look
            worse than yours on a good day.

            CHARLENE *throws up again. Gasping in pain.*

CHARLENE   My throat's on fire.

LUCE   Stinks.

CHARLENE   He was moving?

LUCE   That's his fucking kebab.

CHARLENE   Was he moving?

LUCE	(*Pain of her hand*.) Fucking hell.
	CHARLENE *goes to leave*.
	What you leav– where you, what you doing?
CHARLENE	Going back.
LUCE	Fool, don't be a fool. Look at me. Where's my phone? Get someone to sort this.
CHARLENE	Sort what?
LUCE	Where's my phone! Gimme my phone.
CHARLENE	I ain't got.
LUCE	Gimme my phone.
CHARLENE	I ain't got it.
LUCE	Gimme my phone.
CHARLENE	Your phone's in your arse.
LUCE	Where.
CHARLENE	You fucking.
LUCE	What.
CHARLENE	In your arse.
LUCE	Torched it, we shoulda, shoulda, gimme my phone. That's making me sick. Rank. Your top, your top. Wipe my mouth. What is your stressed – why are you?
CHARLENE	Use your skirt.
LUCE	Look at me.
CHARLENE	We should go hospital.
LUCE	What, you think, what, I'm going, I'm walking in the, some stinky, skanky, skank hospital with MSRA?
CHARLENE	MSRA!
LUCE	Whatever.

CHARLENE   What the fuck!
           This isn't my blood.

LUCE   So.

CHARLENE   Where's this blood come from?
           My fucking head.
           Dj'a reckon someone's found –

LUCE   Who cares.

CHARLENE   Have you got a screw loose.

LUCE   Oh right, right, yeah I see, blame me, yeah.
           This is my fault is it. You're the psycho. You
           always take it too far.

CHARLENE   You give it that, gas it like you're someone –

LUCE   I am someone. I'm fucking, I am, I got, I'm
           starting, starting got a new job –

CHARLENE   You're deluded.

LUCE   Fuck you.

CHARLENE   Fuck you.

LUCE   Fuck off.

CHARLENE   You fuck off.

LUCE   I never asked you – Bane of my, fucking, way
           it's always been. You latch me, you're like a, a
           let, a l- a l-leech – you're like a leech. Follow
           me everywhere –

CHARLENE   Yeah, yeah.

LUCE   Shadow. Have you noticed no one else wants
           you. Like you're no one, everyone has
           abandoned you. Everyone has fucked off and
           left poor little orphan Charlene, like a little
           lonely girl. I've done you a favour. Charity.

CHARLENE   Slag.

LUCE   Look how ungrateful you are.

CHARLENE   Where'd your mum fuck off to?

LUCE   I'd watch it.

CHARLENE   Would you.

LUCE   You don't deserve to be friends with me.

CHARLENE   You ain't my friend.

LUCE   You ain't my friend. I make you look good.

CHARLENE   Seriously I will –

CHARLENE goes for LUCE's throat, they are both all over the place.

LUCE   Psycho! Psycho.

They are struggling and screaming at each other. CHARLENE slaps LUCE.

CHARLENE   You're an ugly cunt.

*LUCE spits in CHARLENE's face.
CHARLENE spits straight back in LUCE's face.*

I will wipe your mouth clean of its teeth. I will wipe your mouth, wipe your fucking face away. I will wipe you out.

You are nothing. You are nothing to me.

CHARLENE exits.

LUCE   Come here and say that. Come here and say that. Oh my god, I can't, my hand, I can't feel my hand. Char. Char! Chaarr!

Twelve

3 a.m. DORIS*'s living room. Suitcase and boxes, tape ready, pile of* LUCE*'s clothes by the door.* LUCE *shoeless and a right mess.*

LUCE	Where am I? Where am I sup– Where do I go? Where do I go!
DORIS	Go to Charlene's. I don't want you here. In this state again.
LUCE	You never wanted me.
DORIS	Don't be silly.
LUCE	You never. What have I done? What have I done?
DORIS	I am sick of this.
LUCE	What have you done this for? What did I do to you?
DORIS	Have you been in a fight?
LUCE	Yeah yeah.
DORIS	Where's Charlene?
LUCE	I'm not her keeper. She's alright. I hurt my hand. It hurts. I don't know what to do. Look at it.
DORIS	What have you done?!
	DORIS *goes and gets a bowl of water and flannel.* LUCE *alone staring blankly into space.* DORIS *enters and tends to* LUCE*'s hand.*
	Can you clench your fist? How have you done this?
LUCE	I don't know.
DORIS	Whenever you are out together, something kicks off with someone and one day you're going to come unstuck... you've got to sort your shit out, Luce, it's ridiculous.
LUCE	I'm ridiculous am I.
DORIS	Your behaviour is ridiculous. You're a thirty-year-old woman.

LUCE	I don't know how it happens.
DORIS	Don't you?
LUCE	Don't don't don't go on at me.
	DORIS *makes a call.*
	Don't phone the police.
DORIS	Do I need to phone the police? (*On phone.*) Hello. Yes, I'm with my daughter, she's blind drunk, and she's burnt her hand somehow. I'm wondering whether I need to take her to A&E... Luce... I have no idea. (*To* LUCE.) How much have you had to drink?
LUCE	How do I know? I don't know.
DORIS	The lady needs to know.
LUCE	A couple of cocktails.
DORIS	She has no idea... She's been out all night, since seven-ish... She's lying on the floor... No, she's thirty... okay sure.
	DORIS *gives* LUCE *the phone.*
LUCE	Yeah... Yeah... What do you mean?... I'm alright, I don't know, he's kicking me out, it's my dad my mum... yeah... yeah... sex on the beach, cocktails cocktails cocktails... vodka... I can walk, I'm walking now... look at the light? Agghhh. Agghhh I feel sick I feel sick...
	LUCE *drops the phone and is retching as though about to be sick.* DORIS *picks up the phone.*
DORIS	...So I don't need to take her to A&E?... Right... No I won't leave her no... right... right... Thank you. Bye.
	Okay I need to keep you warm –
LUCE	Where's my dad gone? Where's my dad. We used to, you used to take me out, you don't come clubbing, you don't take me out any more. You like Char more than you like me. Why do you hate me?

DORIS	Come here.
	DORIS *wraps* LUCE *in a blanket from the sofa.*
LUCE	Do you even like me?
DORIS	I love you.
LUCE	Why do you tell her more than me. I'm your daughter.
DORIS	You don't listen, Luce. You're obsessed with one thing and that's you.
LUCE	I'm sorry. I'm sorry. Alright.
	LUCE *breaks down on* DORIS. DORIS *cradles* LUCE *as though she was five years old, and gently strokes her head.*
DORIS	I've heard it all before, Luce, and I'm tired of this. Therapist said no more stress. I can't have it. Think of other people for once. I need you to change your behaviour.
LUCE	Then I wouldn't be me.
DORIS	It would be a better version of you. I know what you are like under that front and fear. I know you're a good person, Luce.
	When you were born, you were so beautiful you were like a pot of treasure. I'd never known love like it. Beautiful beautiful little girl. Always been a looker, Luce, but you've always been trouble as well. Even at nursery, and I'd go and pick you up, and you'd be scratching other kids' faces because they had a toy you wanted, or kicking someone because they wouldn't play with you, and it was embarrassing.
	Then when they kicked you out of school I thought there's no hope, but you got on, got yourself a little job, always got yourself a job.
	It's not easy being a parent. I sometimes think it's my fault for never really disciplining you. I didn't want you to have my childhood, I wanted

you to be independent, free-thinking, work out
what it was you wanted, follow your own path.

Turn around and my little girl is a woman
but she's still fighting and carrying on. It's got
to stop.

DORIS's *phone rings*.

LUCE   I'm alright.

DORIS   Hello… Yes… Right… right… Tomorrow?…
                We can't see her tonight? Sorry which ward?

Thirteen

Visiting hours

08:30. Hospital. CHARLENE *is in a bed, hooked up. She's had
her stomach pumped.* LUCE *is standing, looking.*

Silence between them. For a long time.

LUCE   Did they stick a tube down you?

CHARLENE   Yeah.

LUCE   Bet you ain't never had something so long in
                your mouth before.

CHARLENE   What do you want?

LUCE   I've forgiven you.

                Silence.

CHARLENE   What's your life plan?

LUCE   What are you on about?

CHARLENE   I was wondering.

LUCE   Live for the day – that's us –

CHARLENE   That's who?

LUCE	Us.

Silence.

CHARLENE	Do you think people should be given a second chance.
LUCE	I've given you enough haven't I.

Beat.

What?

CHARLENE	Go away.

Fourteen

LUCE, PAULO *and* CHARLENE *sat separately addressing audience directly.*

CHARLENE	Pieces ain't piecing together.
PAULO	From where I was.
CHARLENE	What I saw.
LUCE	What I heard.
PAULO	What I saw and heard.
CHARLENE	I can't remember everything.
LUCE	One, two. That's all.
PAULO	They were, excited, off their faces.
CHARLENE	Vodka. Vodka. Wine. Beer. Cocktails.
LUCE	'Bout ten-thirty we left. We were bored. No I didn't lose a shoe.
CHARLENE	One minute we're on the dance floor, next minute we're at the van. He asked me.
PAULO	I get it, with girls, all the time. It happens. All lairy.

LUCE   Thought we'd say hello to Paulo on the way
                home.

CHARLENE   We were just having a laugh.

PAULO   But these two...
                I don't know.
                I don't know who they were.
                She forced her way.

CHARLENE   I don't, I, I don't I don't know. [All] I
                remember is screaming, Luce screaming my
                name. I'm back at the van. I don't know where
                I'd been.

LUCE   He's said to me come here, I've got something
                for you.

                All of a sudden, he's gone mental.

PAULO   Before I knew what there she was, messing
                with my, touching my, provoking me. Asked
                her to leave.

LUCE   He went mental shouting 'get the fuck out of
                my van'. He bangs his fist down.

CHARLENE   I just remember screaming.

LUCE   I've still got the spatula in my hand. He was
                showing me how to flip a burger.

PAULO   Yes I let her in.

LUCE   Screaming in my face, spitting venom, I was
                gobsmacked. He pushes me, I've stumbled back,
                next thing I know he gets me in a headlock.

PAULO   She was really. Confused. Very drunk. Falling
                about. I wanted to call her a taxi. She wouldn't
                let me.

LUCE   He started throwing stuff at me.

PAULO   She just, like that, with her hand, floor covered
                in buns.

LUCE   I couldn't get out, he wouldn't let me out.

PAULO	Yes, I did push her. A push, yes. A slight push. I don't know if it was a push exactly. But the look in her eyes. One of them – the other one said. 'Smash him, smack him.'
LUCE	Hard looks fixed.
CHARLENE	Fists clenched.
PAULO	I just – she just – She crossed a line. Everything I worked for. I work so hard.
LUCE	He threw me, literally threw me to the floor.
PAULO	I fell back.
LUCE	He got my hand. My hand is like – I work with my hands.
PAULO	The smell of burnt flesh.
LUCE	I wanted to get his face and – but I didn't.
PAULO	They pushed my face on the grill.
LUCE	Stunned. Shocked by it.
PAULO	Revolted by my own -
LUCE	Totally shocked.
PAULO	I will smash you up.
LUCE	Stunned. He went for Char next.
PAULO	A surge of rage. Yes.
LUCE	Warm tears. The pain. It was like a –
LUCE	Crack –
CHARLENE	Thud –
PAULO	Whack –
LUCE	He went down.
PAULO	Dazed.
LUCE	I don't know.

PAULO	Broken glass.
LUCE	That was an accident.
	She hit him.
	I don't know how many times.
	Just pummelling.
PAULO	I don't know which one. I was covering my head. Then something was thrown in my face.
LUCE	Came out of nowhere.
PAULO	Didn't see it coming. Burning.

Fifteen

Three months later. Afternoon. DORIS's home. CHARLENE has been three months sober until today's relapse. She is drunk.

CHARLENE	Where is she?
DORIS	Char –
CHARLENE	I wanna know how she's pleading?
DORIS	I think you can guess.
CHARLENE	It weren't just me.
DORIS	I don't doubt it.
CHARLENE	I mean I'm not saying I didn't. I feel fucking awful, can't stop thinking about it. Sometimes the switch flips, sometimes I feel a little bit more together than others. Mostly not. Most of the time I'm on the outskirts, that one foot back.
	I don't know how I did. He was alright. I don't know why I did it. I been trying to work out what happened.
DORIS	You been drinking?

CHARLENE   Course I been drinking.

DORIS   I thought you were sober.

CHARLENE   I just get these mad thoughts, Doris, I'm plotting and obsessing and my mind, it won't stop, got these intrusions from outside, dread from inside. I wanna crawl out of myself.

DORIS   Three months I heard. You were doing really well.

CHARLENE   (*Breaking down.*) Worst three months of my life, Doris. I think I've become more mental. Sorry I don't know why I'm crying I'm always crying. Before I stopped drinking I hadn't cried for about ten years, just felt really fucking sad when I stopped.

Pause.

Been trying to get honest with myself you know, like you did. But here's the difference between me and you. I actually hate myself.

Pause.

And I realised how boring I am, how I didn't have a fucking life plan. I don't know where my life has gone. I don't even know who I am any more and you know what that's frightening. Believe it or not I had... ideas. Yeah. I wanted...

DORIS   You sort this out, you can still do it.

CHARLENE   It's my friend, Doris. Only friend I got.

DORIS   You got me.

CHARLENE   Why ain't you my mum? You're the best mum anyone could have.

DORIS   Right, let's get you home. Sober you up. Get you to bed.

DORIS *gets on her phone to book a taxi.*

CHARLENE   I wanna stop, Doris. I do.

Sixteen

Months later. Court. CHARLENE *is sober.*

CHARLENE   Early morning. I'm emptying my pockets. Not a word, just looks, at me. Scanning me. Testing me. Judging me.

LUCE   I knew I'd set that thing off. Does that detector actually work?

DORIS   Luce.

LUCE   It's big innit. Feel powerful?

DORIS   Come on.

CHARLENE   Again, I'm emptying my pockets. Into the tray. Alone. A cold day. Never imagined this.

LUCE   Why's everyone look so depressed.

DORIS   Court three.

Waiting area outside the courtroom.
CHARLENE *is sat waiting.*

LUCE   Nearly had a heart attack getting here.

DORIS   Thought we were going to be late.

Silence.

(*To* CHARLENE.) How you feeling?

CHARLENE   They're running late.

LUCE   What exactly are we waiting for?

DORIS   Are they. Where's it gone? (*Looking at the screen.*)

LUCE   (*Looking at the screen.*) Are they for real? What are they delaying things for?

Silence as time passes outside the courtroom.

DORIS   All parties called I swear I heard –

CHARLENE   All parties called.

DORIS   All parties called.

LUCE	'Bout time.
CHARLENE	It's so quiet.
DORIS	Stand up.
CHARLENE	In this massive court.
LUCE	Up top have a look, did he just trip up.
DORIS	Ssshh.
LUCE	Probably drunk. This place is a joke. Nothing like *Judge Judy* is it.
DORIS	I am trying to listen.
LUCE	What is he saying? He wants to speak up.
DORIS	They're going through the motions.
LUCE	Blah, blah, blah. The brief gives it that, trying to look all serious. He looks a mess, with his ripped-up cape.
DORIS	It's statistics.
CHARLENE	It doesn't feel real.
DORIS	Nothing about this is real.
LUCE	They wanna hurry up, I'm getting my hair done at two.
CHARLENE	Banging on about.
LUCE	Character –
CHARLENE	Society –
DORIS	Family.
LUCE	Situation –
	Me first. Self-defence. Capable of holding down a job, has prospects. Stable home life. Blah blah blah.
DORIS	But her.
CHARLENE	Me.

LUCE   Her.

CHARLENE   Situation is not ideal, little prospects.

DORIS   Serious.

CHARLENE   Serious.

DORIS   Serious intent?

LUCE   Oh it's very serious.

DORIS   Previous?

CHARLENE   Recklessly causing harm. Damage to property.

DORIS   Pain and suffering.

LUCE   But.

DORIS   In light of.

CHARLENE   All factors taken into consideration.

DORIS   In view of. Showing remorse.

CHARLENE   Banging on about learning skills.

LUCE   Rehabilitation.

DORIS   Treatment.

CHARLENE   Thinking skills.

LUCE   Treatment centre.

DORIS   Probation.

CHARLENE   Numb. Just nothing going on.

LUCE   Compensation to the victim. Fine. Pay that fifty
                  pee a week, laughing.

                  Bang.

DORIS   Bang.

CHARLENE   Bang.

Seventeen

Three months later. CHARLENE*'s bedsit. Very bare. She is*
assembling an Ikea-type wardrobe. Radio on. She is sober.
PAULO*'s face has a big scar down his cheek.*

PAULO	Are you… Do you ever see Luce –
CHARLENE	No.
	Pause.
	What do you want, Paulo?
PAULO	I wanted to…
CHARLENE	I'm meeting someone in five so hurry up.
PAULO	Someone?
CHARLENE	My key worker.
PAULO	I'm leaving today.
CHARLENE	Right.
PAULO	I wanted to know if you want to come with me.
CHARLENE	You need to go.
PAULO	I need to –
CHARLENE	Why aren't you in Russia now, Paulo? Living your life plan?
PAULO	Can I just –
CHARLENE	You were supposed to go what six months ago? Good plan, mate.
PAULO	Will you let me talk.
	Silence.
CHARLENE	Go on then.
PAULO	When I was at college I was struggling. This one morning, I was late getting up and it was right near the end of term and I was already on a warning. My alarm didn't go off and I was just lying there, the sun was really bright burning through my blinds… my body was

aching… and I knew I had to leave. My dad
was no good with words. Words that mattered.
But the words he did use cut deep with short
sentences I'm 'a disgrace', 'not a man', 'let him
down'. His silence was worse. (*Pause.*) For no
reason, he would just… he was a violent man…
I knew if I didn't get out when I did I would
have hurt him. I mean really hurt him… So
I packed my bag, booked a flight.

CHARLENE   What is this about, Paulo?

PAULO   Don't you see there's a way out and I've
forgiven you.

CHARLENE   Oh have you? What and now you're going to
whisk me off to Russia and rescue me. You
think you can just walk back into my life? What
am I gonna do over there, I'm an unskilled
worker with a criminal record, what am I gonna
do, sit at home all day whilst you go out to
work at you're empire, having your dinner
waiting when you get in, play happy families.
Paulo, you don't even know me.

PAULO   I know you better than you think I do.

CHARLENE   You're fucking mental. You shouldn't even
be here.

PAULO   I needed to be sure.

CHARLENE   Sure of what?

PAULO   Your letter. Touched me.

CHARLENE   I had to write that letter. All part of…

PAULO   I know you are different now, now you don't
drink. Things will be different. We could make
a proper go of things.

CHARLENE   Paulo, it's going to take a long time for me to
get things sorted. What you think I just stop
drinking and that's it everything will be alright.
Paulo, you have no idea. I can just about look at
myself in the mirror without hatred. Paulo, I've

been climbing the walls most days, crying myself to sleep, wanting to die.

PAULO   You don't mean that.

CHARLENE   You don't know me.

PAULO   I do.

CHARLENE   You think you do, but you don't.

PAULO   I miss you. Come with me.

CHARLENE   Look at you, Paulo.

PAULO   It's okay.

CHARLENE   How can you say that? To me there's something wrong with you. I can't get my head round... After everything you told me, I think you must like pain. Here's the thing, nothing changes until you make it change. You deserve –

PAULO   We can start over.

CHARLENE   Start over. You'd just be a constant reminder. You're jeopardising my recovery being here. I want you to go.

PAULO   If I give you my address in Russia will you write to me?

               Beat.

CHARLENE   Paulo, go. Go and get on with it. Go and do and get your supermarket, make your millions. I hope business is great, I hope you do it, Paulo. You deserve it.

               PAULO *goes to give* CHARLENE *a piece of paper with his number on it,* CHARLENE *gets on with the wardrobe,* PAULO *places the piece of paper on the floor. He exits.*

               Slow fade to blackout.

               The end.

A Nick Hern Book

Screwed first published in Great Britain in 2016 as a paperback original by Nick Hern Books Limited, The Glasshouse, 49a Goldhawk Road, London W12 8QP

Screwed copyright © 2016 Kathryn O'Reilly

Kathryn O'Reilly has asserted her moral right to be identified as the author of this work

Cover image: Hana Kovacs Photography

Designed and typeset by Nick Hern Books, London
Printed in Great Britain by Mimeo Ltd, Huntingdon, Cambridgeshire PE29 6XX

A CIP catalogue record for this book is available from the British Library

ISBN   978 1 84842 586 6

CAUTION   All rights whatsoever in this play are strictly reserved. Requests to reproduce the text in whole or in part should be addressed to the publisher.

Amateur Performing Rights   Applications for performance, including readings and excerpts, by amateurs in the English language throughout the world should be addressed to the Performing Rights Manager, Nick Hern Books, The Glasshouse, 49a Goldhawk Road, London W12 8QP, *tel* +44 (0)20 8749 4953, *email* rights@nickhernbooks.co.uk, except as follows:

Australia: Dominie Drama, 8 Cross Street, Brookvale 2100, *tel* (2) 9938 8686, *fax* (2) 9938 8695, *email* drama@dominie.com.au

New Zealand: Play Bureau, PO Box 9013, St Clair, Dunedin 9047, *tel* (3) 455 9959, *email* info@playbureau.com

South Africa: DALRO (pty) Ltd, PO Box 31627, 2017 Braamfontein, *tel* (11) 712 8000, *fax* (11) 403 9094, *email* theatricals@dalro.co.za

Professional Performing Rights   Applications for performance by professionals in any medium and in any language throughout the world should be addressed in the first instance to Nick Hern Books (address above).

No performance of any kind may be given unless a licence has been obtained. Applications should be made before rehearsals begin. Publication of this play does not necessarily indicate its availability for amateur performance.

Woodland
CARBON
www.woodlandcarbon.co.uk
NICK HERN BOOKS
Printed on Carbon Captured paper